Edo Architecture:
Katsura and Nikko

Volume 20

THE HEIBONSHA SURVEY OF JAPANESE ART

For a list of the entire series see end of book

Edo Architecture: Katsura and Nikko

by NAOMI OKAWA

with photographs by
Chuji Hirayama

translated by Alan Woodhull
and Akito Miyamoto

New York · WEATHERHILL/HEIBONSHA · Tokyo

This book was originally published in Japanese by Heibonsha under the title *Katsura to Nikko* in the Nihon no Bijutsu series.

A full glossary-index covering the entire series will be published when the series is complete.

First English Edition, 1975

Jointly published by John Weatherhill, Inc., 149 Madison Avenue, New York, New York 10016, with editorial offices at 7-6-13 Roppongi, Minato-ku, Tokyo 106, and Heibonsha, Tokyo. Copyright © 1964, 1975, by Heibonsha; all rights reserved. Printed in Japan.

Library of Congress Cataloging in Publication Data: Ōkawa, Naomi, 1929– / Edo architecture, Katsura and Nikko. / (The Heibonsha survey of Japanese art ; v. 20) / Translation of Katsura to Nikko. / 1. Architecture—Japan—Edo period, 1600–1868. 2. Kyoto. Katsura Rikyū. 3. Nikkō, Japan (Tochigi Prefecture). Tōshōgū. I. Title. II. Series. / NA1553.5.03713 / 722'.1 / 74-23786 / ISBN 0-8348-1027-1

Contents

Edo Architecture:
Katsura and Nikko

CHAPTER ONE

———•———

Katsura and Nikko

IT IS TRULY an exhilarating experience to stand before the Yomei-mon gate of the Tosho-gu shrine at Nikko, surrounded by a crowd of visitors, and listen to the exclamations of wonder evoked by the majesty of the buildings. All around, people are unable to restrain their cries of "How beautiful!" or "How magnificent!" unaware that it is most unusual for traditional Japanese architecture to elicit so direct and emotional a response. At the Katsura Imperial Villa (officially known as the Katsura Detached Palace), however, the reaction of visitors is very different. The atmosphere is hushed and tranquil. Most groups stroll silently through the gardens of this imperial villa, situated on the bank of the Katsura River in Kyoto. They move slowly past the residential buildings and teahouses, uttering hardly a word, carefully measuring their steps as if to engrave their impressions permanently upon their souls.

Why do Nikko and Katsura, as these two complexes of buildings are usually called, elicit such differing responses? Both are classic models of traditional architecture that most Japanese have encountered at one time or another, either directly with their own eyes or in photographs. Both were built at roughly the same time in Japanese history, about 350 years ago, not long after the inception of the age of consolidated feudalism, known as the Edo period (1603–1868) after the seat of the shogunate (modern Tokyo). But despite their contemporaneous construction and their equal rank

as classic expressions of traditional Japanese architecture, the spirit and the aesthetics of Nikko and Katsura are irreconcilably different.

Although built at nearly the same time, the sites and the intended purposes of the two complexes of buildings are quite different. Katsura was built on the outskirts of Kyoto as the villa for an imperial prince's family. Tosho-gu was built north of Tokyo, in the highlands of the Kanto region, as the mausoleum of Tokugawa Ieyasu* (1542–1616), the first shogun of the regime in Edo. But more remarkable is the contrast between the two in the architectural expressions inherent within the buildings.

With unfinished wooden posts and thatched and shingled roofs, the architecture at Katsura embodies unscathed nature; decorative painting and carving are virtually nonexistent. A glance at the buildings' façades (Fig. 8)—sliding wooden-framed screens of translucent paper (shoji), panel doors, and plastered clay walls—immediately reveals how each of the functional elements of the buildings becomes a genuine ingredient of architectural expression. However, at Nikko the architecture is replete with teeming sculptures of dragons, flowers, and birds; and the painted patterns and lacquerwork completely camouflage the basic elements of the structures. The exteriors glitter with gold leaf and bril-

* The names of all premodern Japanese in this book are, as in this case, given in Japanese style (surname first); those of all modern (post-1868) Japanese are given in Western style (surname last).

liant colors—vermilion, blue, and green—so unlike the somber natural hues of Katsura.

The sharply contrasting characteristics of these works of architecture have elicited a bewildering number of questions in relation to an understanding of early modern Japanese architecture, and Japanese culture at large. Few architectural works have undergone as great a fluctuation in aesthetic evaluation and general public reception as Katsura and Nikko. Depending on prevailing tastes and the applicability and adaptability of architectural styles, the Japanese chose one style at one time and leaned toward others at other times.

The appraisal by the German architect Bruno Taut (1880–1938) of Katsura and Nikko left on the minds of Japanese architects a deep impression of the thematic difference between the two works.

Taut visited Katsura the day after his arrival in Japan in 1933. Moved by its beauty, he praised it as a masterpiece, a perfect reconciliation of function and grace, while at the same time dismissing Nikko as "overbearing" and as "novel bric-a-brac."

Reading Taut's commentary on Katsura and Nikko now, we can appreciate it as trenchant criticism rooted in the modern architectural insistence that adornment, a practice hitherto adhered to simply out of inertia, should give way to functionalism, with more respect for the utilitarian aspects of architecture. At the same time, however, we must beware of a certain bias in his attitude, stemming from his ill-considered disregard for tradition. We should read him as representing only a certain trend in architectural history. Particularly

1. *Front Gate and flanking Katsura-gaki bamboo fences. Katsura Imperial Villa.*

doubtful is whether it is valid to judge our entire architectural heritage from the single standpoint of functionalism, because decorative aspects beyond mere expressions of function are beginning to be sought in the works of contemporary architecture. A further problem is that the Japanese appraisal of their own classic structures has been utterly altered in consequence of this one foreign architect's evaluation. For centuries, Nikko has been held dear by the people as a representative work of Japanese architecture. Today, architects and connoisseurs have to prod themselves even to think of going to Nikko—a drastic departure from the practice of the late nineteenth and early twentieth centuries, when Nikko was the scene of apprenticeship for fledgling architects.

Perhaps more important is the question, Are such comparisons of and viewpoints on Katsura and Nikko appropriate in terms of the actual architecture? Various comparisons have been made, such as functional beauty versus decorative excess, natural flavor versus love of gold, and simplicity versus grandeur. But a closer scrutiny of the structures of these two complexes reveals a much broader meaning and fuller expression far beyond such simple appraisals. The structures of Nikko seem, at first glance, to be smothered in gaudy ornamentation, yet the essential architectural skeletons hold considerable force. The elevation of the main sanctuary (Fig. 33), for example, clearly demonstrates the heroic and unwavering strength of its design. Katsura is praised for its simplicity of design, yet there is a considerable amount of variation from one structure to another in the compound, from the

2. *Broad stone-paved approach to Front Gate of Nikko Tosho-gu.*

3. *Stone post reinforcing the latticed-windowed wall, Tamagaki. Nikko Tosho-gu.*

spectacular to the subdued and even to the extremely austere.

What attracts our attention in both cases is the extensive scope of the undertaking. At both Nikko and Katsura, a number of building styles, suitable for different functions, are combined to produce a whole world of architecture where each structure exhibits intense force. Take, for example, the peony sculpture in the Main Hall (Fig. 11) and the phoenix reliefs in the Worship Hall (Figs. 39, 40) at the Tosho-gu shrine, or the interior design of the formal Old Shoin reception suite (Fig. 79) and its surrounding steppingstone arrangements (Figs. 7, 72, 78) at Katsura—all these express a kind of exis-

tential consciousness that transcends aesthetic judgment.

One is awed by the ebullient creative strength of the age that produced Katsura and Nikko; they differ in their form of expression, but both are of epic proportions and powerful design. In what sort of environment and by what sort of people were these two works of architecture built? To find the answer, we must examine the circumstances under which Katsura and Nikko were conceived, the sponsors who gave them life, and the purposes they were intended to fulfill; for only then can we define the meaning that the contrast between these architectural expressions holds for us.

CHAPTER TWO

The Origins

THE PRO-TAGONISTS Plaques with distinguished calligraphy reputedly by the retired emperor Goyozei (1571–1617) are preserved at Nikko and Katsura. The plaque at Nikko (Fig. 26) hangs on the Yomei-mon gate of the Tosho-gu shrine and reads "Tosho Dai Gongen" (Buddha Incarnate, Sun God of the East), a respectful posthumous title for the deified Ieyasu. The plaque at Katsura, placed in one of the gables of the Shokin-tei teahouse, reads simply "Shokin," suggesting that the sound of the wind in the pines (*sho*) nearby is as beautiful as the sound of a koto (*kin*).

Emperor Goyozei acceded to the throne in 1586, the same year in which the military dictator Toyotomi Hideyoshi (1536–98), who had unified the country, became chancellor. This was during the period that saw both the blossoming of the magnificent Momoyama culture (1568–1603) and the zenith of Hideyoshi's power, evidenced by the emperor's unprecedented visit in 1588 to Hideyoshi's Juraku-dai castle-palace in Kyoto. The emperor himself endeavored to foster the new arts and cultural pursuits of the court by patronizing the puppet drama (*joruri*) and by republishing the classic history of ancient Japan, the *Nihon Shoki* (720). The high-minded disposition of the retired emperor, however, occasioned innumerable clashes with the Tokugawa regime. The continuing discord resulted in much chagrin for the emperor, and it was not until the year of his death that he executed the calligraphic plaques for these two architectural monuments.

Nowadays Katsura is known as a "detached palace," or imperial villa, of the imperial family; but originally this villa belonged to the princely family Hachijo (Hachijo-no-miya), later known as Katsura-no-miya. The man who built the villa, Prince Hachijo Toshihito (Hachijo-no-miya Toshihito), was the retired emperor Goyozei's younger brother. Prince Toshihito, who was born in 1579, was called Kosamaru during his childhood. Soon after Emperor Goyozei's visit to the Juraku-dai, the prince nominally entered the Toyotomi family when he was adopted by Hideyoshi. This father-son relationship was abrogated after a son, Tsurumatsu, was born to Hideyoshi. To compensate for this displacement, in 1590 Kosamaru, then just eleven, was created Prince Toshihito, the first to bear the name Hachijo.

In the nearly forty years before his death in 1629, Toshihito, as the head of a most powerful family, rapidly became a central figure in the political and cultural life of the imperial court. His appointment as adviser to Emperor Gomizuno-o (1596–1680), his fifteen-year-old nephew, who succeeded Goyozei, gave him official status; but his high standing at court was due in large part to his excellent education and flawless character. For example, in those times of strained relations between the ruling Tokugawa family and the imperial family, Toshihito played an active role in leadership of the imperial

4. Katsura Imperial Villa as seen across Katsura River.

side, especially in connection with the discord resulting from the entry into court service of Tokugawa Kazuko (1607–78), a daughter of the second shogun, Hidetada, who was later to become consort to Emperor Gomizuno-o.

Furthermore, Toshihito was a seminal force in aesthetic pursuits and was a leading writer of poetry in both the Chinese and Japanese styles. In the literary arts of the day he was guided by Hosokawa Yusai (1534–1610), who was not only a respected warrior and poet but also a tea master and an accomplished literary scholar; and Toshihito inherited from Hosokawa the esoteric exegesis of the ancient poetry anthology *Kokin Waka-shu* (905) that had been handed down from a much earlier age. We also know that Toshihito was well versed in the art of the tea ceremony, already

firmly established by Sen no Rikyu (1520–91) and Furuta Oribe (1543–1615), and that he had a teahouse set up at his mansion for tea gatherings. In addition, he personally directed the arrangements of rocks in his garden. Thus nurtured amid the cultural vitality of the Momoyama court, Toshihito ultimately became the prime exponent of cultural pursuits. From his advantageous position in court, he performed creditably in government work, though he may not have left a visible mark in history.

In 1620, at the age of forty-one, Prince Toshihito set about carrying out plans for a large-scale villa for his own use. His diary entry for June 18, 1620 (by the lunar calendar), records: "[Tokugawa Kazuko] made a bridal entry into court. Shimo Katsura teahouse remodeling under way. Many

5. *The Nikko mountain range; from left to right: Mount Nantai, Mount O-manako, Mount Nyoho. In the middle distance, the cryptomeria forest on the right is the Nikko Tosho-gu area.*

visitors," which reputedly marks the commencement of Katsura villa's construction. This fell on the same date as Tokugawa Kazuko's entry into court as the emperor's consort; the whole town of Kyoto, as well as the court, was filled with enthusiasm for the pomp and splendor of the grand ceremony that was then taking place. Prince Toshihito, who had struggled diligently up to that point, mediating between the court and the shogunate, began to devote more of his attention to the Katsura construction. Abandoning his governmental affairs, he appears to have been determined to withdraw more and more into his own pursuits.

Tokugawa Ieyasu was born at Okazaki Castle, near present-day Nagoya, in 1542 and died when he was 74. Six years younger than Toyotomi Hideyoshi, this leading warrior spent virtually his entire life amid the stormy strife of the Momoyama period, and died in the year following the Summer Siege of Osaka Castle (1615), which marked the fall of the Toyotomi family. That was the sixth year following Emperor Goyozei's abdication in favor of the young Gomizuno-o. The political tenor at the time of Ieyasu's death is reflected in the proscription of Christianity (1613) and in the policies of national fortification (control over daimyo domains, 1614) and of isolation (restriction of trade and closing of ports, 1616–39). This was a period that saw society and culture proceeding toward a yet stricter order of consolidated feudalism.

Ieyasu died on April 17, 1616, in what is now the city of Shizuoka, whence his body was immediately transferred to Mount Kuno on the outskirts

6. *Reliquary-pagoda where remains of Tokugawa Ieyasu
are enshrined. Bronze. Oku-no-in, Nikko Tosho-gu.*

of the city to be entombed until March of the following year. The body was then carried through the various regions of the Kanto district (the area around present-day Tokyo) and finally, on April 4, arrived in Nikko. He was enshrined there in the innermost precinct (Oku-no-in) of the Tosho-gu shrine, which had been under construction since the previous autumn. On April 17 of the same year, the first anniversary of his death, a magnificent transferral-consecration took place at the newly completed sanctuaries of the shrine.

It was in accordance with his last wishes that Ieyasu was first buried at Mount Kuno and then moved to the mausoleum at Nikko. On his deathbed, Ieyasu reportedly told Tenkai (1536–1643), Suden (1569–1633), and an old family retainer: "After I die, I shall first be buried at Mount Kuno in Suruga Province and, after one full year has passed, shall be moved to Nikko. My spirit will abide there, long able to protect my country and my descendants." Several days before his death, Ieyasu had been initiated into esoteric Shinto by the priests Tenkai and Bonshun (d. 1653), apparently indicating his intention to be posthumously deified, following a precedent set by the two great leaders Toyotomi Hideyoshi, enshrined at the Toyokuni Shrine, Kyoto, and Fujiwara no Kamatari (614–69), enshrined at the Danzan Shrine, Nara Prefecture. Ieyasu aspired to be worshiped as a god and revered by the entire nation. The meticulous nature of Ieyasu's instructions concerning his burial place and the formalities of his funeral ceremony was consistent with the character of this man who had laid the cornerstone of the Edo-

7. Stone-paved walkway and steppingstones in front of Mikoshi-yose (Palanquin Approach). Katsura Imperial Villa.

8. Southeastern exposure of shoin *complex; from left to right: New Shoin, Middle Shoin, Old Shoin. Katsura Imperial Villa.*

9. *Katsuradana shelf arrangement, Jodan-no-ma, New Shoin. Katsura Imperial Villa.*

10. *At left, floral openwork pattern on side panel and, at right, decorated panel of door of Kara-mon gate. Nikko Tosho-gu.*

11. *Juncture of Main Hall (at left) and Ishi-no-ma (at right). Nikko Tosho-gu.*

12. *At left, Main Hall, and at right, Worship Hall seen over latticed-windowed wall. 1636. Nikko Tosho-gu.*

13. Sculpted dragons flying above sculpted waves decorating gable of Washbasin Shed. Nikko Tosho-gu.

14. *Demon-faced end tile of Yomei-mon gate. Bronze. Nikko Tosho-gu.*

period feudal system. Moreover, knowing Ieyasu's astute rationalism, unfettered by traditional constraints, we clearly see in the Tosho-gu the foundation of a politically motivated scheme behind this new form of religious architecture.

THE KATSURA PROJECT Shimo Katsura, in southwestern Kyoto, is the site of Katsura Imperial Villa. Originally this land was the resort estate where the Fujiwara, earlier a powerful aristocratic clan, maintained their villa, Katsura Palace. The land later came into the possession of the Konoe, a noble family descended from the Fujiwara; still later, in about 1615, it passed into the hands of the Hachijo family. Prince Toshihito's diary entry for June, 1616, tells of a "melon viewing" excursion to the village of Senshoji, one of his domains across the Katsura River from the present villa, and of strolls along the banks of the Katsura with other nobles, poets, and actors. The area was noted for its melons, and the excursion blended the pleasures of enjoying the company of his friends and of appreciating the melons. From the letters written by Toshihito we know that the retired emperor Goyozei's son Konoe Nobuhiro (d. 1649) and other courtiers were invited to the "little teahouse in the melon fields of Shimo Katsura" to partake of the combined delights of melon viewing and tea appreciation. It is not clear just what the scale of the "little teahouse in the melon fields" might have been, but most likely it was a rest spot provided for use during these excursions.

Current research does not indicate when Prince Toshihito first conceived of a villa or when he began its construction. It may be assumed, however, that the idea took form during the course of his

15. *View of Enrin-do memorial hall showing its arched windows and square steppingstones. Katsura Imperial Villa.*

16. *A variety of bridges at Katsura;* from foreground to background: *earthen bridge in front of Enrin-do, earthen bridge leading to Shoka-tei, and plank bridge connecting Shinsen islets. Katsura Imperial Villa.*

refreshing outings, and that groundbreaking took place in the summer of 1620. Work progressed over the next four years, and in 1624, when the construction and landscaping of the mountain-retreat-style villa were near completion, the first guests were invited. In the summer of the following year Suden, then abbot of the Kyoto Zen temple Nan-zen-ji, was invited to record his impressions of Katsura—the well-known eulogy *Keitei-ki,* which he presented to Toshihito. Transcribed on a plaque, it now hangs on a transom of a room in the Old Shoin complex. It praises Toshihito's character and upbringing: "A gentleman whose heart is pure as the snow, whose words are flowered breezes that blow like captivated benevolence, whose propriety equals that of the Three Huang [legendary Chinese emperors] combined, and whose merits exceed the five Confucian virtues." As for the construction of the villa, the panegyric continues: "In this glorious age, multitudes of workers and hundreds of crafts-men were assembled, brooks dug, hills molded, flowered palaces built, and jeweled pavilions erected." The structures must have presented a delightful appearance indeed, with the satin tex-ture of their fresh cypress timbers glistening softly. "Flowered palaces" and "jeweled pavilions" are perhaps hyperbole, yet creating ponds and hillocks from a wilderness was no mean task. For this rea-son, we surmise that the construction extended over a long period of time and that efforts to compensate for the meager resources of the Hachijo family in-cluded securing financial assistance from the sho-gunate and other sources.

Construction work on the villa was interrupted in 1629 by the death of Prince Toshihito but was later revived, in 1642, by his son Prince Noritada

(d. 1662). Not to be outdone by his father, Noritada devoted himself to the completion of the villa, adding the New Shoin and expanding the gardens. Moreover, special accommodations were erected in preparation for the 1658 visit by Emperor Gomizuno-o, who later returned to Katsura twice. Through the continued efforts of two generations of the Hachijo family during the forty-year period beginning in 1620, Katsura's structures and gardens were finally completed.

The appearance of the villa today faithfully reflects its original form. With the passage of time some buildings have been lost, such as the teahouse Chikurin-tei (Bamboo Grove Pavilion), situated on the bank of the Katsura River, and a vermilion-lacquered bridge in front of the Shokin-tei teahouse; some buildings were later additions or improvements. But it is safe to assume that the build-

ings and landscape remain essentially the same as they were three centuries ago. This is indeed fortunate, inasmuch as gardens and wooden structures are highly vulnerable to the effects of time. Perhaps their preservation can be credited to an early recognition of their precious legacy.

Although research has been conducted on which parts of the villa and its landscape date from Toshihito's day and which were later added by Noritada, no definite conclusions have been reached. It is generally assumed that the Old Shoin complex, the teahouses Shokin-tei and Geppa-ro (Moon-on-the-Waves Pavilion), and their surrounding landscaping belong to the initial phase, while the New Shoin, the Shoi-ken (Beguiling House) teahouse, and their gardens were executed under the direction of Noritada. It also appears that the Miyuki-mon (Imperial Gate) and the Miyuki-michi (Imperial

Path) were additions occasioned by the imperial visits of Emperor Gomizuno-o. The remodeling of the New Shoin's *jodan* (the elevated, seat-of-honor section of a formal reception room) was prompted by the same motivation.

THE NIKKO PROJECT As stated earlier, the construction of the Tosho-gu was nearly complete in the spring of 1617, one year after the death of Tokugawa Ieyasu. The work on the additional structures in the shrine and the efforts to revitalize the affiliated institutions within the Nikko area, such as the Rinno-ji temple and the Futarasan Shrine, continued; and the whole complex was completed around 1619.

Because of the extensive alterations and additions made between 1634 and 1636, which we will consider later, the original appearance of the To-

sho-gu is no longer obvious. Most of the architecture has been completely transformed, leaving untouched only the torii gateway, washbasin, and other stonework. Records dating from the period of construction nevertheless reveal the large scale and extravagant design of the original structures, including not only the main sanctuary and the Honchi-do, or Hall of the Primordial Deity (where Yakushi, the Buddha of Healing, is enshrined as the Buddha of whom Ieyasu was believed to be an incarnation), but also such structures as corridors, an offering hall, a stable for a sacred horse, treasuries, a washbasin shed, and two-story gatehouses, among others.

The distinctive style employed in the main sanctuary is called *gongen zukuri*, an appellation that derives from Ieyasu's posthumous title, Dai Gongen. This style is also known as *ishi-no-ma* (stone

◁ 17. Ama no Hashidate islets viewed from Shokin-tei teahouse. Katsura Imperial Villa.

18. Tea-utensil shelves in Shoka-tei. Katsura Imperial Villa.

room) *zukuri* because the sanctuary consists of a main hall and a worship hall linked in an H shape by a stone-floored chamber, although some *ishi-no-ma* are board-floored. Though known by a different name, this style had been used prior to construction of the Tosho-gu. It had been perfected with the construction of the Kitano Shrine in Kyoto, built during the middle ages for worshiping the martyred scholar-statesman and "god of learning" Sugawara Michizane (845–903), and was employed at the Hokoku Mausoleum (the present Toyokuni Shrine), built to house Hideyoshi's remains. The governing shogunate had earlier destroyed the Hokoku Mausoleum and, in its attempt to arrive at a proper divine appellation for Ieyasu, carefully avoided Hideyoshi's deified name, Hokoku Dai Myojin, instead selecting for Ieyasu the posthumous title Dai Gongen. It would seem, then,

that adopting this architectural style for the Tosho-gu for Ieyasu was not in accord with the shogunate policy of not copying conventions established for Hideyoshi. Apparently the shogunal authorities were unconcerned where the details of architectural styles were at issue, and adopted the *gongen zukuri* simply because the Kitano Shrine, then representative of mausoleum architecture, had followed it. The grand scale of the Kitano Shrine main sanctuary was indeed an ideal model for the Tosho-gu. It may be that the artisans employed, profiting from their experience with the Hokoku Mausoleum, resolved to create an even grander, more flamboyant shrine.

With regard to the style of the decorative details, the contemporaneous Tosho-gu on Mount Kuno and the Futarasan Shrine in Nikko, both extant, suggest that the Nikko Tosho-gu too had originally

19. *Interior of Ishi-no-ma of Kuno-zan Tosho-gu. Mount Kuno, Shizuoka, Shizuoka Prefecture.*

been built in a simpler, more subdued style, not at all resembling its present state, with its overflowing sculptural treatment.

In 1634, eighteen years after its establishment, more large-scale construction was started at the Tosho-gu. Chronicles of the period indicate that this work represents a revival of the ancient practice of periodically rebuilding and rededicating shrine structures. In terms of what was actually accomplished, however, the Tosho-gu undertaking far surpassed reconstruction programs elsewhere, which involved only the duplication of the former structures, as is still done at the Ise Shrine in Ise, Mie Prefecture. Instead, rebuilding the Tosho-gu posed the formidable tasks of redesigning, remodeling, and at the same time expanding to create a totally new shrine.

One factor contributing to the reconstruction of the Tosho-gu at this time was the deep reverence for Ieyasu manifested by the third Tokugawa shogun, Iemitsu (1604–51). We see this in Iemitsu's visits to Nikko to pay homage and in his mandate to select a burial site for him near the Tosho-gu. Iemitsu's sentiments undoubtedly moved the whole shogunate to exert its political and economic power to augment the grandeur of the Tosho-gu.

The decision to refurbish the shrine may also have been motivated by the amazing progress and innovation in architectural design and construction techniques that occurred between 1619 and 1634. Without these developments, there would have been no apparent reason to alter so drastically the overall design of the shrine such a short time after the original construction was completed. Con-

20. *The Tosho-gu main sanctuary viewed from approach to Oku-no-in;* from left to right: *Worship Hall, Ishi-no-ma, Main Hall;* at left in foreground: *Gokuro corridor. Nikko Tosho-gu.*

ceivably behind this reconstruction, which far exceeded the bounds of ordinary repair, was the vigorous architectural creativity during the decade beginning about 1625. The vitality of this period is evidenced by the fact that the shogunate commissioned one imposing project after another—for example, in Edo the construction in 1625 of the Kan'ei-ji temple and in 1632 the mausoleum of Taitoku-in, the posthumous name of the second shogun, Hidetada (1578–1632); and in Kyoto the 1626 remodeling of Nijo Castle, built in 1602–3 as the Kyoto residence of the Tokugawas, and the 1633 reconstruction of the Kiyomizu-dera temple, founded in 798.

Reconstructing the Tosho-gu took a year and a half, from November, 1634, to April, 1636; and on April 17, with Iemitsu present, a grand rededica-

tion ceremony was performed. However, work on the Oku-no-in and minor structures continued until about 1643.

Daimyo who had been hereditary vassals of the Tokugawa and the immediate retainers of the shogun were commissioned to administer the Tosho-gu project, while artisans and artists affiliated with the shogunate were fully mobilized for the task. The supervising administrator was Akimoto Yasutomo (d. 1642), Titular Governor of Tajima (in the north of present-day Hyogo Prefecture), who was later joined by Matsudaira Tadatsuna, Assistant Captain of the Palace Guards. The artisans were headed by Kora Munehiro (1574–1646), Titular Governor of Bungo (present-day Oita Prefecture) and a master builder for the shogunate, who directed the team of his relatives Munehisa, Mune-

tsugu, and Kamenosuke that oversaw the entire construction work. The responsibility for executing the murals and the interior and exterior painting was delegated to the resident shogunate artist, Kano Tan'yu (1602–74). In this effort Tan'yu directed painters both of his own school and of the Hasegawa school, which had earlier branched off from the Kano school. The artists distributed among themselves the task of painting dragons, each differing in shape, on the coffers of the Worship Hall ceiling; and thus these panels bear on their backs the signatures of such famous artists of the day as Tan'yu and Kuzumi Morikage. Top-ranking craftsmen also lent their energies to the lacquerwork, *maki-e* (lacquerwork with embedded or inlaid gold or silver dust), and metal forging and casting.

The scale of this reconstruction project is known in detail from the *Tosho-gu Gozoei-cho,* the account book kept by the Akimoto family and submitted to the shogunate. The vast undertaking included the main sanctuary, the Kara-mon with its undulating Chinese-style gables, the latticed-windowed walls (Tamagaki) around the main sanctuary (Fig. 30), the corridors, and the Yomei-mon gate, among other works—some thirty structures in all, encompassing the entire precincts of the Tosho-gu we see today. In addition, the work required impressive civil-engineering feats to improve the approach to the Oku-no-in complex, as well as to erect the stone fence near the Front Gate and to set the gigantic stone foundation on which rest the corridors flanking the Yomei-mon gate. The project also entailed relocating the Honchi-do building to a site in the

21. *View of the Taiyu-in main sanctuary;* from left to right: *Worship Hall, Ai-no-ma, Main Hall. Taiyu-in.*

22. *Wall decoration above hinged door at juncture of Worship Hall and Ai-no-ma;* from top to bottom: *shrimp-shaped beam, phoenix and Chinese-lion medallions, transom decoration. Taiyu-in.*

Kan'ei-ji and razing some thirty other structures dating from the original construction.

Altogether this ambitious project cost the shogunate some 568,000 *ryo* in gold currency, 800 pounds of silver, and 5,000 bushels of rice. This outlay undoubtedly represented a considerable portion of the shogunate's military treasury. In manpower, the project required 1.69 million man-days of work by carpenters and their assistants, 23,000 man-days of gold-leaf application, and 2.83 million man-days of cartage. If we calculated the cost of 4.5 million man-days by present-day standards, even at a conservative $25 per day the labor alone would amount to the staggering sum of more than $100 million.

Tosho-gu today still fairly accurately presents its final form achieved during the reconstruction. The basic architecture and sculpture are known to date from this period, and while the exposed decorations have been repainted or refinished in subsequent repairs, the original design and style are thought to remain unchanged. Some later alterations included replacing the cypress-bark roofing on the Main Hall, Worship Hall, Kara-mon, Yomei-mon, and Sakashita-mon with bronze-tile roofing in 1654, and removing part of the north corridor around 1650 when the stone retaining wall behind it was strengthened. Originally there were no pagodas at the Tosho-gu, but in 1643 the Sorinto pagoda was built within the Oku-no-in precinct. In 1648 this tower was removed, and a five-story pagoda was placed in the Tosho-gu forecourt, near the torii gateway. However, this pagoda was destroyed by fire in the early 1800s, and the existing

23. *The Taiyu-in Washbasin Shed, whose roof is supported by granite pillars.*

version dates only from 1817. Another fire, on March 15, 1961, destroyed the roof and interior decoration of the Honchi-do; and restoration was carried out from 1962 to 1967. Therefore, although the structural members and exterior ornamentation of the Honchi-do date from the original construction, the interior is a modern reproduction.

In 1653, seventeen years after the completion of the major reconstruction work on the Tosho-gu, the Taiyu-in, the mausoleum of Tokugawa Iemitsu, was built in Nikko. (Taiyu-in was Iemitsu's posthumous name.) As in the case of the Tosho-gu, the construction was carried out under shogunal auspices. The Taiyu-in project was administered by Heinouchi Masakatsu, Titular Governor of Osumi (in the eastern part of present-day Kagoshima Prefecture), who was, with Kora Munehiro, a shogunal master builder. Kano Tan'yu was again

charged with responsibility for the murals and overall painting of the buildings.

Although the layout of buildings and the architectural styles of the structures at the Taiyu-in are much like those at the Tosho-gu, there are many features that reflect the trends of a new age. A marked difference is seen in the Taiyu-in Main Hall, which, because of Buddhist services performed there, is patterned after the Buddha hall usually found in a Zen monastery; whereas the Main Hall at Tosho-gu exemplifies typical Shinto-shrine architecture. The superbly crafted Taiyu-in, along with the Tosho-gu, remains an outstanding Edo-period work of religious architecture. In view of the design accomplishments evident at the Taiyu-in, we will take another look at how the architecture of Tosho-gu was transformed by a later generation.

24. *Drainage spout set into stone wall. Nikko Tosho-gu.*

CONTRASTS IN ORIGIN Both Katsura and Nikko were conceived in the 1610s, and in the space of the following forty years their construction proceeded concurrently. These works are indeed contemporaries, but the circumstances surrounding their origins are remarkably different.

First and foremost, the Tosho-gu represented religious architecture, a mausoleum for the Tokugawa shogun who had only recently achieved political dominion over Japan; but Katsura was a retreat for a princely family that had already lost real political power. Furthermore, Nikko is politically inspired architecture, emanating from Ieyasu's desire to ensure both his own place in history and the succession of his heirs; Katsura is the architecture of refined delight, born of the highly cultivated character of Prince Toshihito. In their

separate spheres, both Katsura and Nikko stood out as architectural monuments of the day.

Another contrast worthy of note is the disparate approach to choosing the sites. In the Heian period (794–1185), during the days of imperial rule, Katsura was the site of the retreats of the courtiers Minamoto no Takaakira (914–82) and Fujiwara no Michinaga (966–1027). In the chapter "Matsukaze" (The Wind in the Pine Trees) of the eleventh-century novel *Genji Monogatari* (The Tale of Genji), there is a detailed description of a scene at Katsura in which the protagonist, Hikaru Genji, gazes at the moon while enjoying the music of flutes and lutes. In Heian times Katsura was famous for its beautiful view of the moon and appeared often in the poetry of the imperial court. Prince Toshihito once compiled a collection of quotations from ancient poems that took Katsura as their theme. From

25. Triangular steppingstone in front of Shokin-tei teahouse. Katsura Imperial Villa.

his thorough knowledge of classical literature, he was very familiar with the history of Katsura's signal importance to the imperial court. Undoubtedly the strength of long tradition coupled with Katsura's proximity to Kyoto, then the imperial capital, influenced Toshihito's selection of the site for his villa.

In contrast, since ancient times the Nikko mountain range, lying at the periphery of the Kanto Plain, has been a focus of mountain-spirit worship. Generations of itinerant Buddhist monks meditated there, amid the stark natural setting. The atmosphere of Nikko is vastly different from the traditional, imperial splendor of Katsura, nestled in the milder Kyoto climate.

Interestingly enough, Ieyasu had never visited Nikko, though he chose it as his burial site. He seems to have heard of it from his attendant Tenkai, then the abbot of the Rinno-ji, and accepted Tenkai's recommendation because of Nikko's reputation as a sacred place revered throughout the ages by the people of the Kanto region. Earlier, on an assignment from Hideyoshi, Ieyasu entered the Kanto region, and with surprising alacrity and resolution he chose the marshes of Edo, which he had never seen, as his base of operations. Possibly, in his selection of Nikko, we detect the same political boldness inherent in the shrewd Ieyasu. These considerations stand in sharp distinction to the tradition-steeped origins of Katsura.

26. Front of Yomei-mon gate with guardian deities sitting on both sides of entrance. Nikko Tosho-gu. (See also Figures 27, 56.)

27 (overleaf). Yomei-mon gate and its ▷ flanking corridors. Nikko Tosho-gu.

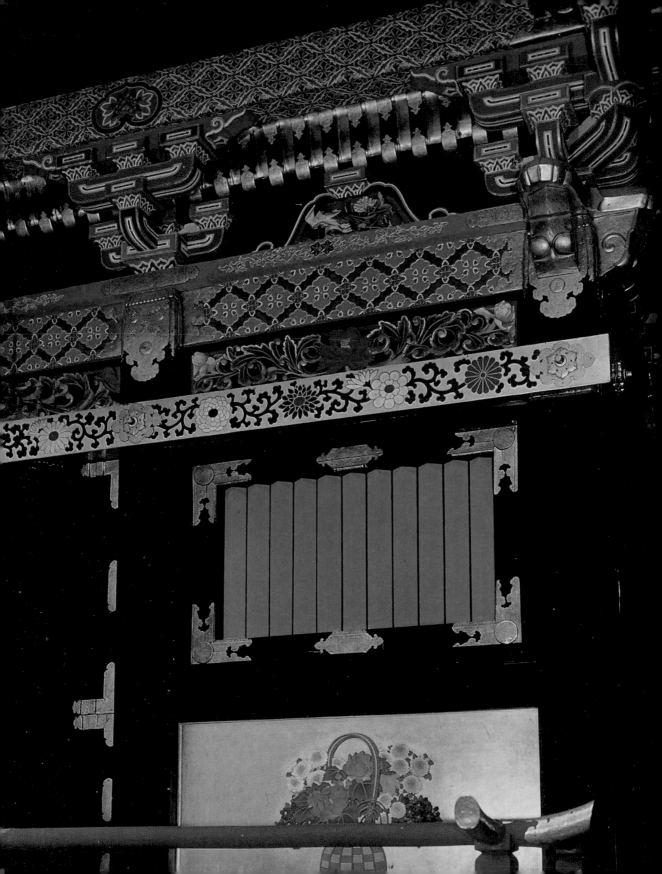

◁ 28. *Bracketing and decoration of Kagura-den;*
notice use of black lacquer and contrasting wall
painting on a gold ground. Nikko Tosho-gu.

29. Karahafu *gable and bracketing of Shin'yo-sha. Nikko Tosho-gu.*

30 *(overleaf). Worship Hall seen beyond Kara-mon gate. Nikko Tosho-gu.* ▷

31. *View of Kara-mon showing end gable. Nikko Tosho-gu.*

32. *Sculpture, gold, and lacquerwork decoration on ▷ underside of eaves of Kara-mon gate. Nikko Tosho-gu.*

33. *Western exposure of Main Hall. 1636. Nikko Tosho-gu.*

34. *Decorative sculpture in gable of Main Hall. Nikko Tosho-gu.*

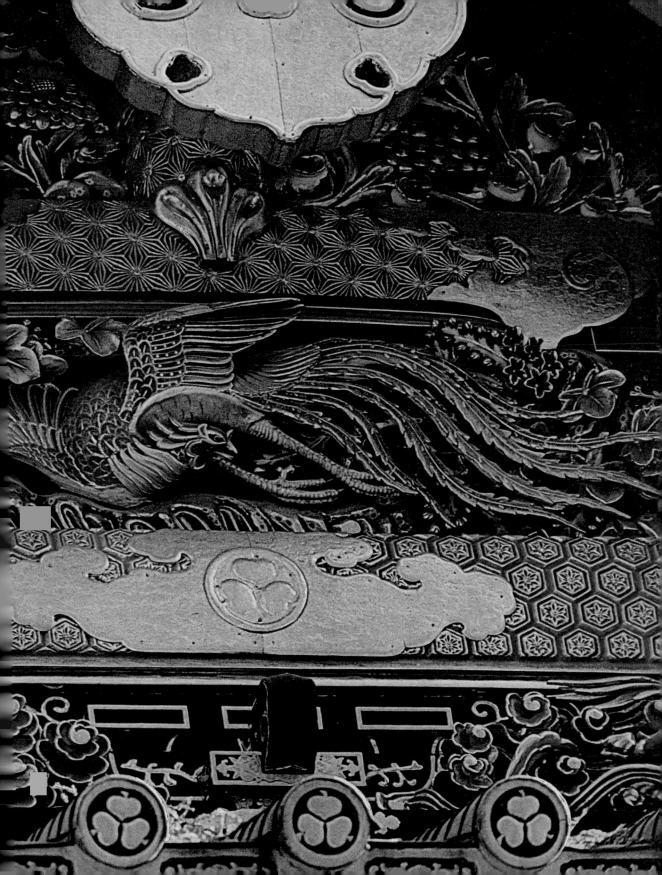

35. *Northwestern exposure of Main Hall. 1653. Taiyu-in.*

36. *Juncture of Ai-no-ma (at left)* ▷
and Main Hall (at right). Taiyu-in.

37. *Sculpture of* baku *(imaginary dream-eating animal) on Front Gate. Nikko Tosho-gu.*

38. *Sculpture of Chinese lion on* ▷
Yomei-mon gate. Nikko Tosho-gu.

39. Interior of Shogunal Chamber, Worship Hall. Nikko Tosho-gu.

40. Detail of assembled sculpture of phoenix and pau- ▷
lownia tree seen in third panel from left in Figure 39,
Shogunal Chamber, Worship Hall. Nikko Tosho-gu.

41. *Interior of Gokuro (corridor to Ishi-no-ma). Nikko Tosho-gu.*

42. *Hinged door of Ai-no-ma at* ▷
juncture of Worship Hall. Taiyu-in.

43. *Front Gate seen through stone torii gateway. Nikko Tosho-gu.*   44. *Approach to Oku-no-in precinct. Nikko Tosho-gu.* ▷

45 *(overleaf). Sacred Bridge over Daiya* ▷
River at entrance to Nikko area. 1636.

CHAPTER THREE

The Design

THE TOSHO-GU On entering the Tosho-gu complex, one first becomes aware of an intricately juxtaposed, multilayered spatial organization. Unlike the predictable geometric arrangements of structures on open, level ground found at ancient Buddhist temples, at Nikko the path from the Front Gate to the Yomei-mon and on to the Kara-mon and the main sanctuary winds, bends, and rises with each level of stone stairs, the gates and flanking structures revealing themselves in planned asymmetry. As one progresses along the path, one finds that one piece of architecture after another presents a new form: sparsely decorated and sedate; strangely sculpted; ominously soaring; unpainted residential style; and finally, through the Kara-mon—dusted with vermilion *maki-e* and ornamented with pure white sculpture—the golden gables and glistening eaves decorations of the Main Hall come into view.

Briefly, the spatial arrangement of the Tosho-gu consists in several open squares defined by stone walls and steps, linked by the path leading to the main sanctuary, with buildings placed along this approach. Because the Tosho-gu precincts are carved out of a mountain slope and this of itself dictates a relatively rigid spatial distribution, a further deliberate series of variations in layout, style, and coloring of the buildings is employed. Distinct types of architecture abound: the precincts within the Front Gate alone have twenty-two separate structures, each with a unique style and deco-

ration. The enticing power of the Tosho-gu is in its total synthesis of architectural design, which unfolds like a gigantic picture scroll.

The architecture of the Tosho-gu is purported to represent the *kara-yo*, or Chinese style (an intricate formalistic idiom also known as the Zen style after its abundant use in Zen monasteries), but with the addition of varicolored, heavy, and exaggerated decoration. Some liken Tosho-gu's architecture to the Western baroque. Yet the initial visual impact on entering the precincts is one of forthright architectural composition and a serene classical expression.

THE FRONT GATE. At the entrance to the Tosho-gu compound is the Front Gate (Fig. 46), which houses two statues of the Benevolent Kings (Nio), hence its name Nio-mon. This gate is in the *hakkyaku-mon* (eight-legged gate) style, so called because at both front and back of the gate there are four supporting pillars, or "legs," making a total of eight (Fig. 47). This style was often used in the massive gates of ancient temples, as exemplified by the East Main Gate of Horyu-ji and the Tegai-mon (Harm-changing Gate) of Todai-ji, both in Nara Prefecture. The Front Gate's double-beam gables and, in the interior, its M-shaped ceiling, called the *mitsumune zukuri* (three-ridge construction), are details patently copied from traditional temple gates. The posts, beams, and bracketing to support the eaves are, as is common in this style, packed tightly together and generously proportioned.

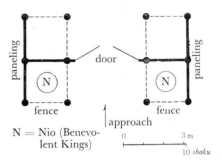

46, 47. Left, *side view of Front Gate showing sculptures of Chinese lions,* baku, *and chrysanthemums on beam ends and peony sculpture inside gable;* below, *ground plan. Nikko Tosho-gu.*

paneling

paneling

door

N

N

fence

fence

approach

N = Nio (Benevolent Kings)

0   3 m

10 *shaku*

48. Front view of Middle Treasury. Nikko Tosho-gu. ▷

In contrast with the structural framework, the sculpted lions, elephants, *baku* (imaginary demons said to eat dreams), and peonies on the ends of the beams offer astonishing variety and lavish coloration. Sculpted within the gables are large chrysanthemums, and painted on the ridgepole and beam surfaces are flower diamonds, Indian swastikas, *tatewaku* (undulating-line motif) and other brightly colored motifs. This expressive and elaborate ornamentation, masterfully harmonized with the bold construction, results in a display of strength unique to the Front Gate.

THE TREASURIES. Upon entering the Front Gate, straight ahead one immediately sees the Middle Treasury (Fig. 48), flanked by the Upper (Fig. 49) and Lower treasuries. The Middle Treasury faces

the part of the sacred path that makes a left turn just before reaching the treasuries. Built in the raised-floor style with walls similar to the traditional *azekura* (the so-called log-cabin-style storehouses), these buildings house such treasures as the historical costumes for the thousand-man procession, an annual festival for which the Tosho-gu is well known.

The gently sloping hipped-and-gabled roof of the Middle Treasury presents a low, calm profile. The treasury, measuring nine bays in length, is divided into three chambers, each with a door in its middle bay. This floor plan is imitative of the ancient paired-storehouse style, in which two *azekura* are linked by a hall, as exemplified by the Shoso-in repository of the Todai-ji. The decorative

details of the Middle Treasury inherit those of the traditional *wa-yo* (Japanese style) design, a style predating the *kara-yo*, which was not imported from China until the Kamakura period (1185–1336). The wall decoration is simple, devoid of sculpture, and is limited to painted arabesque designs of peonies. This faithful execution in the *wa-yo* style, which characterizes the stateliness and refinement of traditional Shinto architecture, distinguishes the design of the Middle Treasury.

The Upper and Lower treasuries differ considerably from the Middle Treasury in external appearance, as well as in decorative details. For example, the huge, soaring gables are enclosed in the steep, high-rising hips of the gabled roofs; and it is the end walls that squarely face the sacred path. These façades are composed of twisted, bulky beams and bottle-shaped posts characteristic of the *kara-yo;* and they are decorated with large carvings of elephants in the arches of the gables, as well as demons on the lower ends of the posts, so that the appearance of these gargoyled treasuries is fearsome indeed. In the structural details too, in contrast with the relaxed, harmonious design of the Middle Treasury, the use of verdigris-colored frog-crotch struts—inverted-Y-shaped ornamental brackets—lends a further sense of lavishness. In this uninhibited and atypical style the builders' spirit of creativity and unrestricted expression is vividly portrayed.

THE SACRED STABLE. Immediately after entering the Front Gate one sees on the left the stable where

49. *The Upper Treasury. Nikko Tosho-gu.*

the sacred horse used on ceremonial occasions is housed (Fig. 50). The only unpainted structure in the entire precincts, it is renowned for the colorful "hear-no-evil, see-no-evil, speak-no-evil" monkeys carved in a panel on the façade. The building departs from the typical architectural forms of temple and shrine stables and is executed in a style more similar to the formal residential style of feudal lords' mansions. Inside, opposite the comfortable box stall for the horse there is an attendants' waiting room. This fact, together with the general floor plan of the structure and the style of the tack and trappings, recalls the stables and equipment that appear in Momoyama-period folding screens depicting daimyo mansions in and around Kyoto. The square, unpainted timber posts, found nowhere

else at the Tosho-gu, also attest to the use of a residential style in this stable.

The extended-eaves-style roof, the exterior façade of unpainted timber, and the black-lacquered lattice doors generate a quietly elegant aura conspicuous among the myriad brightly hued buildings within the compound. This intentional accent of the Sacred Stable in the precincts, achieved through the application of a residential style, may indeed be acclaimed as an excellent example of the designers' creativity.

THE WASHBASIN SHED. In the west corner of the forecourt, a short distance from the Sacred Stable, stands the Washbasin Shed (Fig. 52). Its large *karahafu*-gabled roof (using the Chinese gable, with undulating bargeboards, a flattened central arch,

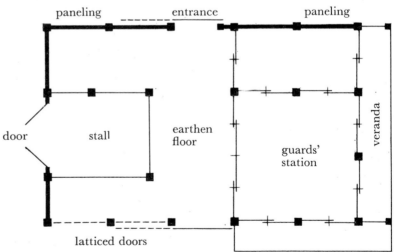

paneling   entrance   paneling

door   stall   earthen floor   guards' station   veranda

latticed doors

50, 51. The Sacred Stable (above) and its floor plan (right). Nikko Tosho-gu.

0   3 m

10 *shaku*

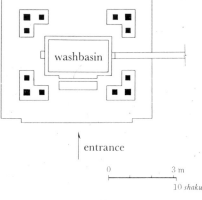

52, 53. *The Nikko Tosho-gu Washbasin Shed (left) and its plan (above).*

and trailing ends) is supported by stone pillars. Similar large-canopied Chinese- or *karahafu*-gabled roofs were much favored during the Momoyama period, and this washbasin shed too echoes the expansive mood of that society. However, the use of cut stone for the corner pillars was a novel innovation.

This shed shelters the large granite basin that provides fresh water for the necessary ritual rinsing and purification of hands and mouth before entering the shrine's inner precincts. Dragons cavorting above ocean waves, symbolic of the basin water below, are carved into a panel in the arch of the gable, and exquisite peonies and dragons are painted on the cambered beams. All this endows the architecturally compact shed with a majestic opulence.

The washbasin is one of the oldest of its kind in Japan: from the beginning it has supplied water through a siphon system with underground pipes. Water for ritual purification at other shrines had almost always had its source in natural streams or wells. The technique used at the Tosho-gu skillfully incorporated the technical advances in plumbing systems evidenced in castle and town building of the period.

THE SACRED BRIDGE. As with the Washbasin Shed, the Sacred Bridge (Fig. 45), which spans the Daiya River below the Nikko area, deserves attention as an exemplar of the application of new technology. Well-known among historic bridges in Japan, this arched bridge with lacquered balustrades appears to be no different from the typical Japanese bridge

54. Sculpted panels on outer wall of corridor flanking Yomei-mon gate. Nikko Tosho-gu.

in the indigenous style except for its unique girders. The girders are firmly embedded in the river embankment, the weight of the structure transferred to the girders by means of crossbeams, with massive granite piers lending additional support.

A bridge already existed on this site during the middle ages, greatly predating the Tosho-gu shrine. The present structure is attributed to the period of shrine reconstruction in the 1630s, when the bridge was also remodeled. The original bridge was simply an arch supported by wooden girders. (An extant example of this earlier bridge style is the Saru-hashi bridge in Yamanashi Prefecture, one of the "Three Eccentric Bridges of Japan.") This bridge was improved upon by adding stone supporting columns. The technique of strengthening a bridge with stone

pillars is mentioned in records relating to bridge construction over the Kamo River in Kyoto during the Momoyama period. This technique is one of the achievements of construction technology that was probably developed during the active period of castle building.

It is worth noting that at the Tosho-gu the traditional architecture in the native *wa-yo* style, as seen in the Washbasin Shed and the Sacred Bridge, has been augmented by innovations in both waterworks and structural techniques, creating an unprecedentedly forthright architectural vocabulary.

The structures between the Front Gate and the Yomei-mon include the Lavatory, Sutra Repository, Bell House, Drum House, and Honchi-do.

The architecture of these buildings is in the typical Buddhist tradition, and they are generally arranged in the *kara-yo* style, which is rather calculated and cold.

Thus the outer precinct of the Tosho-gu displays an array of twelve structures contrasting both in purpose and in style. It is evident that the organization of diverse buildings and the play of contrapuntal styles define the thematic plan of the Tosho-gu. This method of contrast in design finds further repetition in the three exquisite structures within the courtyard inside the Yomei-mon: the Kagura-den (Sacred Dancing Stage), the Shin'yo-sha (Portable-Shrine Storehouse; Fig. 55), and the Shrine Office. Here we see a wealth of contrasting variation in roofs, ornamental details, and color

schemes, which are fully discussed in chapter six.

THE CORRIDOR AND THE SACRED WALL. The architecture within the Yomei-mon is dramatically unlike that of the outer precinct; the space arrangement of the outer buildings shifts to a dense composition, and the style and ornamentation rise to new heights of elaboration. This inner sanctum, defined by a latticed-windowed sacred wall (called Tamagaki, or "jewel fence") and surrounding corridor, focuses on the main sanctuary and contains the Yomei-mon, Kara-mon, and a small group of buildings including the Shin'yo-sha. The practice of encircling a sanctuary with a double enclosure composed of fence and corridor was not traditional: most ancient temples had only a surrounding corridor, while shrines had an encircling fence with a

◁ 55. The Shin'yo-sha (Portable-Shrine Storehouse). Nikko Tosho-gu.

56. The Yomei-mon gate. Nikko Tosho-gu. (See also Figures 26, 27.)

corridor on only the front side. The combined use of both fence and corridor to produce a stately inner courtyard dated only from the time of the Hokoku Mausoleum (1598), dedicated to Toyotomi Hideyoshi.

At the Tosho-gu in particular, through use of the brilliant leaf-shaped latticework in the sacred wall, the tortoise-shell patterns on the horizontal beams, and the extensively sculpted panels along the corridor (Fig. 54), the builders succeeded in creating around the Main Hall a spatial quality hitherto unknown. Today, as we traverse the makeshift path cutting through the latticed-windowed wall to enter the Main Hall, no remnant of this spatial arrangement can be discerned. Originally, however, there was a north side to the present corridor, enabling

one to walk the entire length of the corridor and view the main sanctuary from all sides through the latticed windows. Even now, as we tread the gravel in this courtyard, we can savor the noble mass of the Main Hall and its orderly and colorful beauty glimpsed between the brilliant patterns of the sacred wall.

THE YOMEI-MON AND KARA-MON. The Yomei-mon and Kara-mon gates are located at the front of the corridor and at the sacred wall, respectively. They are encrusted with decoration and, per square foot of construction, undoubtedly cost far more than any other structure in the whole compound.

Structurally, the Yomei-mon is a three-bay-wide, two-story-high gatehouse (Fig. 56). Its details, such as the radiating rafters, bracketing system (Fig. 57),

57. *Bracketing of Yomei-mon gate. Nikko Tosho-gu.*

and balustrades, are all in the *kara-yo* style. The use of sculpture is particularly distinctive, since almost none of the ends and faces of the beams, brackets, and panels are left unsculpted. The Kara-mon (Fig. 58) is not a typical Chinese-style gate, as is indicated by the strong curve of the gables and the strange shape of the beams, by the inlaid sculpture in rare wood on the surfaces of the posts and door panels (Fig. 60), and by the deeds of the legendary Chinese emperor-sage Shun depicted in carvings on the transoms (Fig. 59). There are two other Chinese-style gates at the Tosho-gu—one behind the Main Hall and the other at the entrance to the mausoleum in the Oku-no-in precinct—but neither exhibits the complex ornamentation of the Kara-mon.

Thus in both structure and decoration the Yo-mei-mon and the Kara-mon aim to achieve an intricate, elaborate, and strikingly novel expression. For a deeper understanding, we should here analyze further the design methods employed.

The structural framework of both these gates is in the *kara-yo* style. Chinese-style gables are affixed to the roof; however, they are not designed with the orthodox camber found at the Washbasin Shed but, instead, show a powerfully arched profile. Sculpture is employed to the full: the motifs include auspicious birds of Chinese origin and weird animals, such as phoenixes, dragons, and lions, as well as depictions of people famous in Chinese legends, all to the exclusion of Japanese motifs and themes. In the color scheme, white, black, and gold are domi-

58. *The Kara-mon gate. Nikko Tosho-gu.*

nant; the subdued colors common to Japanese taste, which are seen at the Kagura-den, are carefully avoided.

It is frequently claimed that the Yomei-mon and the Kara-mon are elaborate examples of the *kara-yo,* the architectural style of Zen Buddhism. But as we can see, what was attempted here was a foreign or Chinese decorative effect. The appellation *kara-yo* has long been applied to diverse art styles, but basically it referred to new modes imported from China. In the past, since China had been the sole foreign country from which culture was transmitted to Japan, the term *kara-yo,* by extension, also connoted "foreign" or "quaint." It is evident that the craftsmen who designed these two gates sought to create an exotic image. Given the milieu of the time,

however, what the designers managed to produce did not represent the Chinese reality; rather, it was a reflection of the designers' imagination. A similar attempt was repeated in modern times: in the early years of the Meiji era (1868–1912), when there was an influx of Western culture into the country, Japanese architects rushed to build in the Western style, but the buildings they designed were in fact nothing more than amalgamations of different Japanese architectural styles of the time.

Though the builders of the Yomei-mon and the Kara-mon had aimed at a *kara-yo* effect in both, the two works are quite different in expression. The Yomei-mon is executed faithfully in the *kara-yo* tradition and, with its abundant sculpture, makes a forceful, expressive impression. In contrast, in the

Kara-mon attention is focused on the bold, unconventional shapes of the structural framework. The difference in expression in these two gates attests to the creativity of the designers. In terms of conceptual daring the Kara-mon is more notable, and this may be the reason that many consider the Kara-mon to be of superior design.

THE MAIN SANCTUARY. To summarize the attributes of its architecture, the main sanctuary employs all the architectural forms we have seen up to this point: the abundant sculpture, the lavish inlay, the decorative *maki-e*, and the unrestrained use of color. Within the sacred wall, the sanctuary rises in epic proportions, high above the granite foundations on which it firmly rests, unfolding the entire span of its immense roofs. The carved chrys-

anthemums between the bracket complexes supporting the veranda (Fig. 33), the brightly colored phoenixes carved in the transoms, the white posts and ornamental beams laced with designs in gold, the black brackets decorated with gold arabesque designs and lines and with carved dragons and *baku* on the ends, the wildly colored arabesque patterns under the eaves and sculpted phoenixes in the gables—all this ornamentation on the building creates the impression of a lavishly decorated picture scroll opening before one's eyes.

Inside, the principal section of the Worship Hall is flanked by the Shogunal and the Cloistered Prince's chambers, whose walls are embellished with murals of phoenixes and hawks inlaid in rare wood (Fig. 39) and whose ceilings are decorated

59. Sculpture on Kara-mon gate: bas-relief aquatic plants seen above frieze of the legendary Chinese emperor-sage Shin and his courtiers. Nikko Tosho-gu.

60. Assembled bas-relief sculpture of dragon on post of Kara-mon gate. Nikko Tosho-gu.

61. Main sanctuary seen over latticed-windowed wall; at left, Main Hall, and at right, Worship Hall. Nikko Tosho-gu.

with minutely sculpted chrysanthemums. Here is powerful ornamentation far transcending that of any other building in the compound.

The floor plan of the main sanctuary (Fig. 62) is in the H-shaped *gongen zukuri* style and consists of the nine- by five-bay Worship Hall and the five- by five-bay Main Hall, linked by a stone-floored chamber, the Ishi-no-ma. The Tosho-gu main sanctuary is the largest structure in the *gongen zukuri*. A large-scale *gongen zukuri* structure using round posts, such as this sanctuary, was described by the architects of the Edo period as grand-scale *gongen* construction in the *kara-yo* style.

To a great extent we can think of the *gongen zukuri* of the main sanctuary as being in the *kara-yo* tradition. For example, the simple rounded capitals

of the posts, the moldings on the ends of the head beams, the ornamental balls on the railing posts, and the bracketing all represent the *kara-yo*. But there are details that cannot be identified with the *kara-yo*: the parallel arrangement of rafters deviates from the radiating style of the *kara-yo*; the top-hinged latticed windows of the Worship Hall and the shoji and panel doors on the veranda of the Main Hall are all elements of the traditional *wa-yo*. The construction of the sliding partitions of opaque paper (*fusuma*) and of the ceiling in the interior of the Worship Hall is quite similar to the distinctively Japanese *shoin*, or formal residential, style. The main sanctuary, therefore, is built on a principle completely different from that of the pure *kara-yo* style of the Yomei-mon.

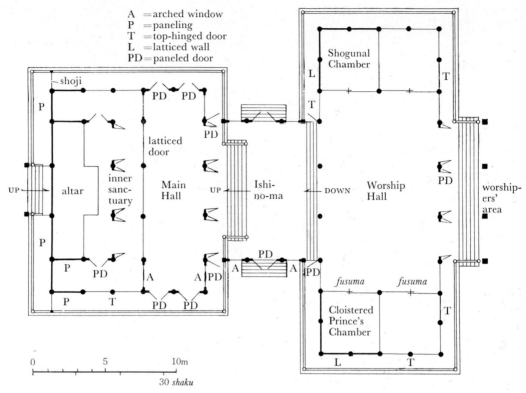

A = arched window
P = paneling
T = top-hinged door
L = latticed wall
PD = paneled door

shoji

P

PD   PD

PD

latticed
door

inner
sanc-
tuary

Main
Hall

altar

UP

P

P

P
PD

A   A PD

P   T   PD   PD

0   5   10m

30 *shaku*

Ishi-
no-ma

UP

DOWN

PD

A   A PD

L

Shogunal
Chamber

T

T

Worship
Hall

PD

worship-
ers'
area

PD

fusuma   *fusuma*

Cloistered
Prince's
Chamber

T

L   T

62. *Floor plan of main sanctuary. Nikko Tosho-gu.*

The choice of motifs and decorative techniques is also different from that of the Yomei-mon. For example, in addition to the weird animals and auspicious birds, such as dragons, lions, *baku,* and phoenixes, the themes for the sculpture and painting include a number of purely Japanese subjects, such as waterfowl and chrysanthemums. The colors are not simply white, black, and gold but include a combination of primary colors.

Both in structure and in ornamentation, an unfettered sense of design is evident in the execution of the main sanctuary. Indeed, the central objective of this monumental undertaking, as explicitly revealed here, was to pursue the full range of expressive idiom to create a place of worship on an impressive scale.

The heavily ornamented main sanctuary may very well repel a viewer more accustomed to the architecture of simplicity, such as that at Katsura. Yet as one appreciates the sanctuary from the graveled courtyard or walks from the Shogunal Chamber to the Ishi-no-ma and to the Main Hall, it becomes apparent that the whole design of the sanctuary manifests an expressive intensity and force greatly superior to the later examples of architecture that merely continued using ornamentation tritely. The powerful dragons sculpted under the corner eaves of the Main Hall (Fig. 33), the full-blooming peonies carved above and below the curved beam in the wall connecting the Ishi-no-ma and the Main Hall (Fig. 11), and the sharp-eyed look of the phoenix fixing its prey on the wall of the

THE TOSHO-GU · 75

63. *Niten-mon gate. Taiyu-in.*

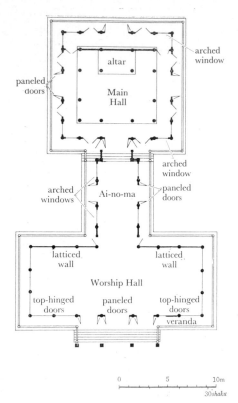

64. *Floor plan of main sanctuary. Taiyu-in.*

Shogunal Chamber (Fig. 40)—all these express a vigorous energy rare in Japanese architecture. These reliefs were all created with a freedom unhampered by conventions of form or color.

The architectural adornments of the main sanctuary may at first glance appear to be independent of or even in disunity with the structural scheme. However, it is more accurate to say that the ornamentation and the structural style collide with great force. Indeed, it is in this rival tension and vigor that we find the main sanctuary's stirring expression.

THE TAIYU-IN   The layout of buildings in the compound at the Taiyu-in mausoleum is basically taken from that of the Tosho-gu.

The arrangement from the Nio-mon (Front Gate) through the Treasury, the Washbasin, and the Lavatory to the Bell House and the Drum House, as well as the plan of a latticed-windowed sacred wall and a corridor around the main sanctuary, copy those of the Tosho-gu, though on a somewhat smaller scale. This similarity is quite natural in light of the fact that the mausoleum was built for the enshrinement of Tokugawa Ieyasu's grandson Iemitsu.

A careful inspection of the ground plan, however, reveals the incorporation of many new elements not found at the Tosho-gu. In comparison with the Tosho-gu, the Taiyu-in has a narrower breadth, and its corridor extends only across the front of the precinct. But the architecture along the

65. *Northwestern exposure of Main Hall. Taiyu-in.*

central axis is more complicated in design. For example, a two-story gatehouse, the Niten-mon (Fig. 63), is placed between the Nio-mon and the Yasha-mon (corresponding to the Yomei-mon); at the entrance to the Oku-no-in stands the Koka-mon, built in the Chinese style, with a whitewashed arch (Fig. 66). Furthermore, the path linking these gates twists and turns, and overflows with stone steps. (See foldout opposite page 60.)

Taking the path from the Nio-mon to the Oku-no-in, one initially feels that the Taiyu-in is richer in variety and more fascinating in design than the Tosho-gu. On closer scrutiny, however, one finds that the grand structural composition and the spectacular, extensively landscaped development of the Tosho-gu compound is lacking here. What we are presented with at the Taiyu-in is a more delicate and intricate approach to architecture.

Among the structures at the Taiyu-in, the majority of the auxiliary structures lack inherent expressive powers and therefore are not stimulating; but the Otama-ya (Fig. 65), the main sanctuary, is undeniably superior in design and craftsmanship. This structure resembles the Tosho-gu *gongen zukuri* in general plan (Fig. 64), since it encompasses the Main Hall, executed in the style of a Zen Buddhist hall, and the Worship Hall, which are linked by the Ai-no-ma. However, unlike the Ishi-no-ma at the Tosho-gu, the Ai-no-ma is neither stone-floored nor a step lower than the other buildings; and the two-story Main Hall actually mirrors the appearance of the "founder's hall" in a Zen temple.

66. Koka-mon gate at entrance to Oku-no-in precinct. Taiyu-in.

In style, the Otama-ya represents the delicacy and complex technical niceties of the *kara-yo*. In the balanced proportions of the façades, in the precise curvature of the eaves, and, where the eaves of the Main Hall and the Ai-no-ma meet, in the finely curved beams supporting narrow rafters (Fig. 36), the masterful design is visible beneath the ultimate technical achievement of the Edo period. The basic color of the ornamentation is gold, as is evident in the carvings on the door panels and in the swallow-tail patterns on the slightly convex surface of the decorative timber above the lintels. The design of the brackets beneath the veranda, with gold leaf applied to the beveled edges of each member, skillfully creates a subtle beauty.

The overall composition of the Taiyu-in's Main Hall differs considerably in its expression from that of its counterpart at the Tosho-gu, albeit the same decorative themes are often repeated. For example, let us compare the treatment of the walls that connect the Ishi-no-ma (or Ai-no-ma) with the Main Hall and the Worship Hall, because this particular element characterizes the design of the *gongen zukuri*.

The *kokabe* (transomlike wall) of the Tosho-gu Main Hall is actually a beam boldly curved like a rolling wave and adorned with Chinese-style lion and peony sculptures (Figs. 11, 121) seemingly bursting from the confines of the beam. In contrast, the corresponding *kokabe* at the Taiyu-in has beams that are curved gently if at all, and the sculpture is neatly contained: an extremely polished design.

67. *Eaves bracketing of Koka-mon gate. Taiyu-in.*

Where the walls of the Ai-no-ma and the Worship Hall meet (Fig. 42), several phoenixes in crestlike motifs distributed on a patterned ground impart an air of elegance. However, at the Tosho-gu the sculpture overpowers the structure.

From even this brief comparison it is apparent that the overriding power inherent in the sculpture and color at the Tosho-gu did not repeat itself at the Taiyu-in: emphasized in its place are technical and decorative refinement. Furthermore, at the Taiyu-in the compositional planes of the wall surfaces and patterns take priority over the sheer volume of the buildings.

The same trend is observable in other structures in the Taiyu-in compound. For example, the builders of the Koka-mon were quick to adopt the style

of the Dragon King's palace, a design then freshly imported from Ming China (1368–1644). With its delicate composition the Koka-mon gives the illusion of an architect's replica rather than an actual building. In the corridor and the walls beside the Niten-mon and Nio-mon, a fretwork pattern is employed, cleverly alternating vermilion frets on a black ground with black frets on a vermilion ground (Figs. 68, 69). This is a drastic departure from the lively trail of sculpture around the corridor at the Tosho-gu.

The phantasmagoric profusion of carved lions, elephants, *baku*, peonies, and chrysanthemums scattered about the Front Gate at the Tosho-gu is absent at the Nio-mon (the front gate of the Taiyu-in), leaving only the uniformly stern-faced Chinese

68. *Side wall adjoining Niten-mon gate. Taiyu-in.*

69. *Side wall adjoining Front Gate (Nio-mon). Taiyu-in.*

lions. From this comparison we can see how rigorously the architectural expression at the Tosho-gu, born as it was of unrestrained fantasy, reflected and adhered to the mood of early Edo society and how rapidly, within the few decades before the Taiyu-in was completed, this climate and force receded into oblivion.

KATSURA The Katsura Imperial Villa is not vast, as one soon discovers by walking through the grounds. There are far fewer buildings here than at the Tosho-gu. As one proceeds along the visitors' path, passing through the connected quarters of the Old, Middle, and New *shoin* complexes, then descending into the garden, walking around the hillocks and the pond, past the Geppa-ro, Shokin-tei, Shoka-tei, and Shoi-ken teahouses, all of Katsura has been seen. Yet after only one tour of its architecture and landscape, we become vividly aware of manifold impressions. Even if we attempt to recall those separate buildings and parts of the garden that had particularly impressed us, the sheer richness of the diversity makes any such attempt futile.

In accordance with the landscaping conventions of the time, which aimed at enhancing the expanse of nature, Katsura's man-made pond inlets and miniature hills are intricately interwoven to create a feeling of depth. But the grandeur we observe at Katsura does not stem merely from this artificially created natural scenery. Above all else, what strikes us most profoundly at Katsura is the diversity of

70. *Garden and pond viewed from Ni-no-ma, Old Shoin. Katsura Imperial Villa.*

71. *Garden viewed from Gakki-no-ma. Katsura Imperial Villa.*

72. *Stone walkway and steppingstone arrangement beside the moon-viewing platform, Old Shoin. Katsura Imperial Villa.* ▷

74. Northern exposure of Shokin-tei teahouse. Katsura Imperial Villa.

◁ *73. Southwestern exposure of Shokin-tei teahouse. Katsura Imperial Villa.*

75. *Tokonoma of Ichi-no-ma, Shokin-tei teahouse. Katsura Imperial Villa.*

76. Interior of ceremonial tearoom, Shokin-tei teahouse. Katsura Imperial Villa. (See also Figure 88.)

77. Garden viewed from Ichi-no-ma, Shokin-tei teahouse. Katsura Imperial Villa.

78. *Steppingstone arrangement in garden south of Old Shoin. Katsura Imperial Villa.*

79. *Interior of Ichi-no-ma, Old Shoin. Katsura Imperial Villa.*

80. Side window of tokonoma, Ni-no-ma, New Shoin. Katsura Imperial Villa.

81. Interior of Pantry, New Shoin. Katsura Imperial Villa.

83. *Interior of Geppa-ro teahouse. Katsura Imperial Villa.*

◁ 82. *Interior of Shoi-ken tea-*
house. Katsura Imperial Villa.

84. Stone-paved walkway leading to washbasin and stone lantern beside waiting booth. Katsura Imperial Villa.

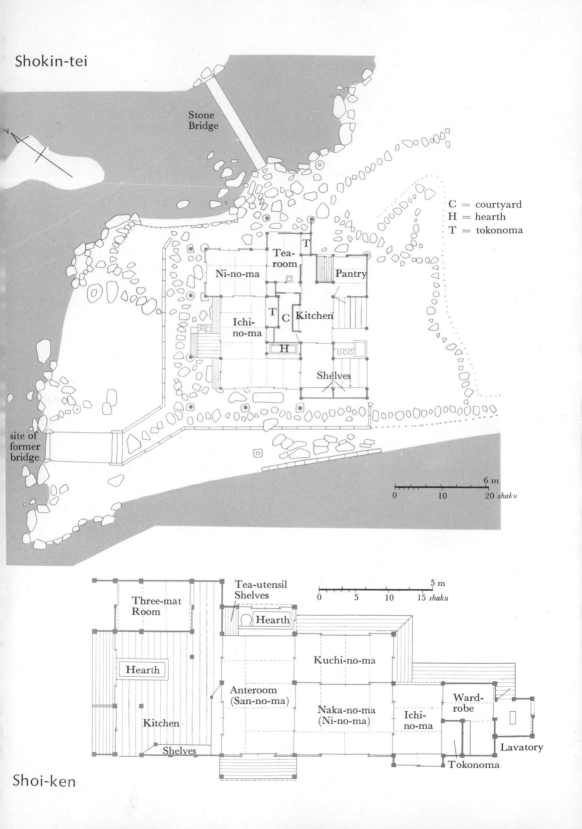

Shokin-tei

Stone
Bridge

C = courtyard
H = hearth
T = tokonoma

T

Tea-
room

Ni-no-ma

Pantry

T

Ichi-
no-ma

C Kitchen

H

Shelves

site of
former
bridge

6 m

0   10   20 *shaku*

Three-mat
Room

Tea-utensil
Shelves

5 m

0   5   10   15 *shaku*

Hearth

Hearth

Kuchi-no-ma

Anteroom
(San-no-ma)

Naka-no-ma
(Ni-no-ma)

Ichi-
no-ma

Ward-
robe

Kitchen

Lavatory

Shelves

Tokonoma

Shoi-ken

Manji-tei

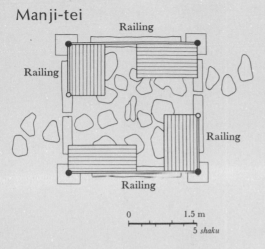

Railing

Railing

Railing

Railing

0   1.5 m

5 *shaku*

Shoka-tei

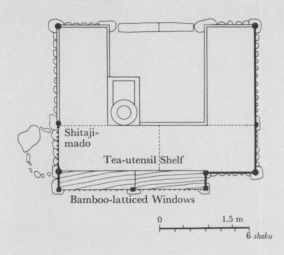

Shitaji-
mado

Tea-utensil Shelf

Bamboo-latticed Windows

0   1.5 m

6 *shaku*

Enrin-do

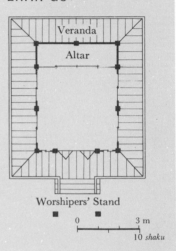

Veranda

Altar

Worshipers' Stand

0   3 m

10 *shaku*

Tea-Ceremony Waiting Booth

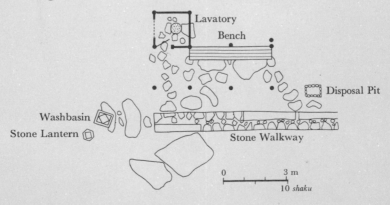

Lavatory

Bench

Disposal Pit

Washbasin

Stone Lantern

Stone Walkway

0   3 m

10 *shaku*

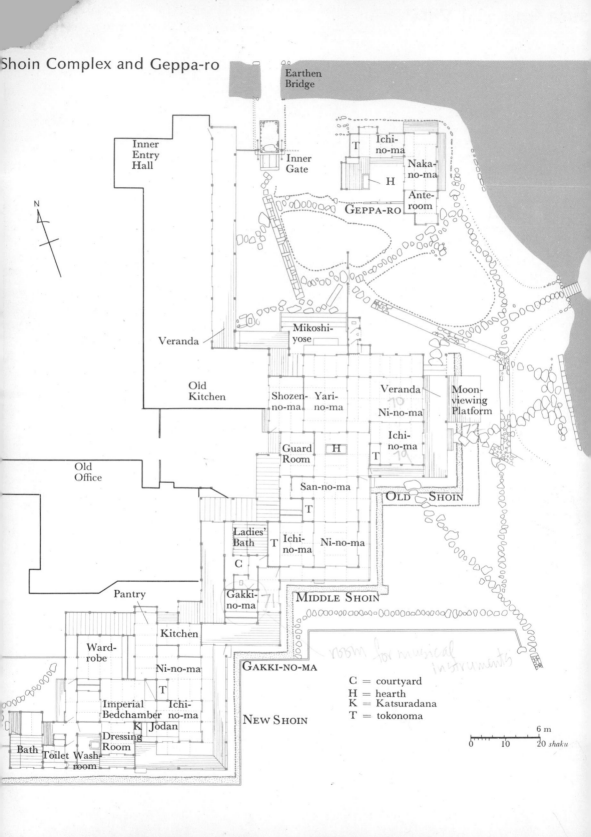

Shoin Complex and Geppa-ro

Earthen Bridge

Inner Entry Hall

Inner Gate

GEPPA-RO

Ichi-no-ma

Naka-no-ma

Ante-room

T

H

Veranda

Mikoshi-yose

Old Kitchen

Shozen-no-ma

Yari-no-ma

Veranda

Ni-no-ma

Moon-viewing Platform

Ichi-no-ma

T

Old Office

Guard Room

H

OLD SHOIN

San-no-ma

T

Ladies' Bath

T

Ichi-no-ma

Ni-no-ma

C

MIDDLE SHOIN

Gakki-no-ma

Pantry

Kitchen

Ward-robe

Ni-no-ma

GAKKI-NO-MA

room for musical instruments

T

Imperial Bedchamber

Ichi-no-ma

K Jodan

NEW SHOIN

Dressing Room

Bath

Toilet

Wash-room

C = courtyard
H = hearth
K = Katsuradana
T = tokonoma

6 m

0   10   20 shaku

Katsura Imperial Villa

Ground Plan

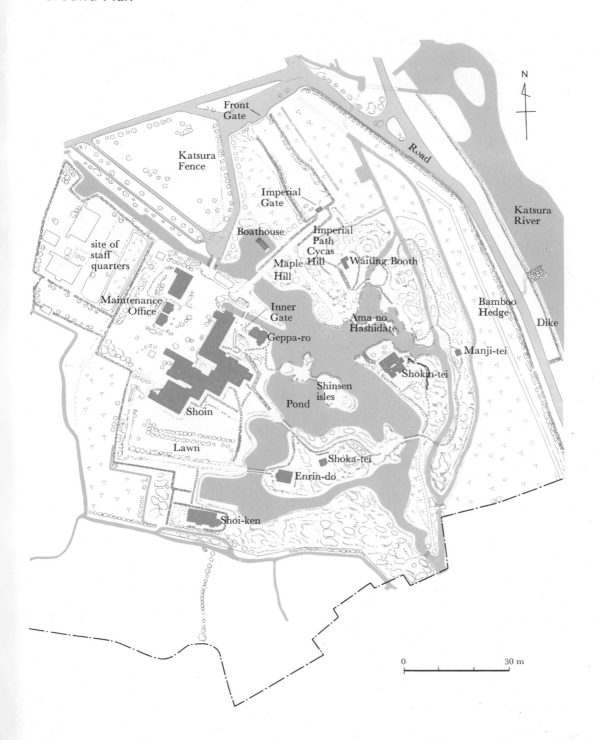

Front Gate

Katsura Fence

Imperial Gate

Boathouse

site of staff quarters

Imperial Path

Cycas Hill

Maple Hill

Waiting Booth

Road

Katsura River

Maintenance Office

Inner Gate

Geppa-ro

Ama no Hashidate

Bamboo Hedge

Dike

Manji-tei

Shokin-tei

Shinsen isles

Pond

Shoin

Lawn

Shoka-tei

Enrin-do

Shoi-ken

N

0   30 m

85. *Tokonoma and* chigaidana *of Ichi-no-ma seen from Ni-no-ma, Middle Shoin. Katsura Imperial Villa.*

expression in the architecture and landscaping: no design or pattern is ever repeated here.

THE OLD AND THE MIDDLE SHOIN. Admiring the "orthodox steppingstones" (Fig. 7), that is, the path formed by neatly embedded slabs of stone, we enter the Old Shoin complex at the Mikoshi-yose, the entrance where the palanquins of visiting noblemen were once set down. (See foldout opposite page 96.) Inside, we behold the simple yet expansive spatial composition. Instead of ornate decoration, the large rooms of nine, ten, and fifteen tatami (rice-straw mats), partitioned by wide *fusuma,* have simple narrow lintels, unassuming transoms, and ordinary ceilings supported by wooden slats. On the southernmost side of the Old Shoin, facing the pond, there is a room with a plain toko-

noma alcove (Fig. 79). A veranda is attached to the room, and a moon-viewing platform made of bamboo (Fig. 70) extends beyond the veranda.

Sitting in a tatami-floored room of the Old Shoin, one commands a good view of the garden, consisting of the pond in the foreground, the Shinsen islets in the middle, and the cryptomeria-covered hillock beside the Shokin-tei teahouse in the distance—all framed in the crisp outline of the shoji panels and transom. The orientation of the room, as the name "moon-viewing platform" would suggest, is in the direction of the moonrise. Conceivably it was designed specifically as a terrace for moon and garden viewing. Judging from the existence of one large, fifteen-mat room and another with an *irori* (sunken hearth) in its center, the Old Shoin was intended

86. *Ornamental fittings on* chigaidana *in the Ichi-no-ma, Middle Shoin. Katsura Imperial Villa.*

to accommodate a number of people at informal gatherings.

The Middle Shoin appears stiff and stern, in complete contrast with the lighthearted, relaxed feeling of the adjoining Old Shoin. At one end of the L-shaped room arrangement in the Middle Shoin is a tokonoma the full width of the room, and to its right, in the adjoining wall, is a *chigaidana*, a staggered group of ornamental shelves. On the walls of the tokonoma and *chigaidana* and on the *fusuma* are *sumi-e* (ink paintings) of landscapes and the Seven Sages of the Bamboo Grove (third-century Chinese literati who engaged in "pure conversation," transcending worldly concerns). In comparison with the Ichi-no-ma in the Old Shoin, which appears rustic because of its plank doors, the Middle Shoin Ichi-no-ma imparts the air of a

formal sitting room. From the grace and dignity of its chambers, it may be inferred that the Middle Shoin was built as living quarters for Prince Toshi-hito himself. This is further evidenced by a bath and a toilet installed at the rear of the Ichi-no-ma. A veranda about three feet wide ran along the two sides of the Middle Shoin that face the garden. Now covered with tatami, it was originally made of plain boards. This former veranda leads to a room called the Gakki-no-ma (room for musical instruments), where *biwa* (lutes), koto, and other instruments were stored on special shelves. At the rear of the room is a broad veranda, probably built so that the prince could enjoy music while commanding an excellent view of the garden (Fig. 71).

The adjoining complexes of the Old and Middle Shoin and the Gakki-no-ma are believed to be the

87. *Stone lantern at tip of cobblestone peninsula. Katsura Imperial Villa.*

oldest part of Katsura. Functionally, these structures must have played a central role in the compound, as can be inferred from the presence of large guest rooms and the prince's living quarters. But the architectural expression of what was intended to be the focus of Katsura is surprisingly simple. The exteriors consist simply of plank doors and shoji, arranged apparently with no effort to embellish or to display craftsmanship.

In the interior and exterior appearance of these *shoin,* however, we perceive an unconstrained yet forceful and cohesive atmosphere. No technical accomplishment in these buildings attracts our special attention, but, as witness the delicate qualities of the Old Shoin veranda, the content and purpose of the architecture is forthrightly reflected in the simple design. It is worth noting that the

focus, and therefore the essence, of the entire villa is designed in such an artless, unassuming idiom.

SHOKIN-TEI. Opposite the Old Shoin across the pond lies the teahouse Shokin-tei, the principal structure in the garden in terms of size, as well as location. From its sitting room one commands an overall view of the garden: the stone bridge (Fig. 112), the rocky shoal (Figs. 74, 87), and the bridge-connected islets called Ama no Hashidate (Bridge of Heaven; Figs. 17, 77) on the right-hand side; the Shinsen islets in the center (Fig. 155), the gently sloping lawn dotted with small pine trees, and the cryptomeria-covered hill beyond the turbid pool on the left-hand side.

The Shokin-tei is fashioned in the style of a *minka* (rustic residence of the common people); its thatched roof extends over an earthen-floored area,

88. Interior of ceremonial tearoom, Shokin-tei teahouse, showing windows, nijiri-guchi (guests' entrance), and tokonoma. Katsura Imperial Villa. (See also Figure 76.)

89. Shinsen islets viewed from Ni-no-ma, Geppa-ro teahouse. Katsura Imperial Villa.

forming broad eaves. The hearth for boiling tea under this canopylike roof gives the cottage the air of a wayside resthouse. Once inside, however, especially in the Omote-no-ma (Ichi-no-ma), one finds the interior design unexpectedly proper and dignified. The sturdy square posts, the austere tokonoma, and the well-proportioned transom are all assembled by a disciplined hand.

The design of the Omote-no-ma is basically the simple *shoin* style, discussed in relation to the Old and the Middle *shoin*, with the incorporation of the feeling of natural materials that is found in the *soan* (rustic hermitage) style of teahouses. The use of natural materials is exemplified by the wicker door between the veranda and the Ni-no-ma and by the transom between the Ichi-no-ma and the Ni-no-ma (shown in the upper left-hand corner of Figure 75),

which is made of hemp stalks. The Ni-no-ma also features several gourd-shaped *shitaji-mado* (latticed window in a plastered wall; Fig. 157), often seen in the *sukiya zukuri*, or teahouse style of architecture. Thus the design of the Shokin-tei as a whole is keyed to the decorum of the classic *shoin* style; moreover the famous blue-and-white Ichimatsu (checkerboard) pattern on the tokonoma wall (Fig. 75) and the admixture of elements of the *sukiya* style create a feeling of gaiety.

The Shokin-tei was intended as a pavilion for such entertainments as moon viewing, poetry contests, and music appreciation, and in this capacity excels any other structure in the villa. Originally a large vermilion-lacquered bridge connected the front of the Shokin-tei with the footpath stretching from the Imperial Path. It is surmised that on the

occasion of his visit to Katsura the retired emperor Gomizuno-o strolled across this bridge to reach the teahouse, where he enjoyed his leisure.

The tea-ceremony room (Fig. 76) adjacent to the Ni-no-ma offers a contrast with the serene atmosphere of the Omote-no-ma. A *sanjo-daime*— that is, a tearoom with three tatami and a *daime* (a three-quarter mat for the host)—the room is designed in perfect harmony with the proper tone of the *soan* style. Inside, the *shitaji-mado*, the ceiling, and the *naka-bashira* (the "central post," which is the hearth-side end post of the extended wall in front of the *daime*) are all arranged with delicate sensitivity. This room is familiarly called the Yatsu-mado Kakoi (eight-window tearoom) because of its many windows and has long been known as the "first and foremost in the style favored by Enshu."

We do not know whether Kobori Enshu (1579–1647), the celebrated tea master and garden designer, actually designed this particular tearoom. However, compared with other tearooms in whose design Enshu definitely had a hand—such as the Hasso no Seki (which also means "eight-window tearoom"; Fig. 114) in the Konchi-in, a subtemple of the Kyoto Zen temple Nanzen-ji—a similar taste is manifest throughout, as in the technique of placing one window above another over the low *nijiri-guchi* ("wriggling-in entrance," that is, the guests' entrance) and in the skillful overall composition using many windows and entrances (Fig. 88).

This is the only authentic ceremonial tearoom in the villa, and no doubt the tea ceremonies that Prince Toshihito performed as host took place here. The lengthy approach leading from the Imperial

90. *Southwestern exposure of Geppa-ro teahouse. Katsura Imperial Villa.*

Path to this teahouse was designed as a *roji* (tea garden), a large landscaped area comprising the waiting booth, the Cycas Hill, a cascade, a rocky shoal, and the Ama no Hashidate islands, all arranged with great ingenuity. Great care was also taken with the placement of stone lanterns.

The Shokin-tei is an architectural work incorporating a dual spatial character: a grand parlor for lively entertainments and a restful tearoom of rustic simplicity. One, located to command an unhindered view of the limitlessly spacious garden, suited the elegant life style of the nobility, heirs to the traditions of the imperial court. The other, placed at the very end of the passage that connects the austere rock arrangements in the tea garden with the rigidly restricted interior, was ideal for the

spiritual enlightenment sought in the tea ceremony. The harmonious combination of these rooms of differing characters required special efforts. This is reflected in their layout and in the small inner court provided in the interior of the house. This courtyard, which one does not discover until well into the building, is a contrivance one cannot surmise from the roof, which maintains its beauty and unbroken line when viewed from any angle.

GEPPA-RO. Atop the high stone retaining wall facing the pond to the left of the palanquin approach to the Old Shoin is the teahouse Geppa-ro (Fig. 90), literally, the "Moon-over-the-Waves Pavilion." As with the Old Shoin, the shoji and the bay windows open toward the moonrise so that one can, as the name suggests, gaze at the moon-

91. *Northern exposure of Shoi-ken teahouse. Katsura Imperial Villa.*

rise across the pond beyond the neatly dressed hedge. Inside the Geppa-ro (Fig. 83), the sitting rooms are arranged in an L shape around an earthen-floored area, which has a wooden-floored section, a hearth, and shelves—all the equipment necessary for a tea gathering or a small party.

With regard to the interior design, the roof deserves particular attention: excepting the Ichi-noma, which is the main guest room, none of the rooms has a finished ceiling; instead, the underside of the woven bamboo-and-rush roof is left exposed. The bark has not been stripped from the logs used for the king posts and the beams supporting the weight of the roof. While this use of an unfinished ceiling probably derived its inspiration from the ceilingless earthen-floored room of the traditional

farmhouse, the drastically restricted use of beams and posts makes for a refreshing, pleasant space free of commonness.

SHOI-KEN. Unlike the Geppa-ro, which in its shingled roof retains the refined flavor of a nobleman's retreat, the Shoi-ken teahouse (Fig. 91) appears to be an exact replica of a farmhouse. In contrast to the similarly thatched Shokin-tei, whose hipped-and-gabled roof lends it considerable formality, the Shoi-ken has merely a simple hipped roof. The low, projecting lean-tos further identify the structure with the farmhouse tradition.

The south side of the Shoi-ken is only six meters from the bamboo fence marking the boundary of the villa. Just beyond the fence, fields are still cultivated today. From the Shoi-ken sitting room

92. *Veranda and bamboo mullions of San-no-ma, Shoi-ken teahouse. Katsura Imperial Villa.*

one can look through the bamboo mullions of the veranda (Figs. 92, 158) and watch people at work in the neighboring fields. When the wind comes from the right direction, the rich smell of earth permeates the teahouse.

Besides structures like the Shokin-tei and the Geppa-ro that were intended primarily for the pastimes of the nobility, such as moon viewing and poetry recitals, the garden architecture at Katsura also included structures, such as the Shoi-ken, that were built near the edge of the property to permit one to savor the delights of rural nature and life. For example, near the banks of the Katsura River there was originally a teahouse called the Chiku-rin-tei, from whose rooms one could enjoy the spectacle of fishermen catching small river trout.

The type of architecture found in the Shoi-ken was contrived essentially to produce the appearance of a farmhouse, in keeping with the surrounding rustic scenery. On the side of the Shoi-ken facing the fields, the natural roofline, the bamboo-lined veranda, and the latticed windows above the shoji are all deceptively characteristic of a peasant house. The bamboo-mullioned screen on the outer edge of the veranda strikes even the modern eye as a work of fine craftsmanship, but it used to be a common fixture—called the "lion window"—in every rural house; it was designed to keep out predators like wild dogs and foxes. This practical farmhouse device is adopted here in its pure form.

Inside the Shoi-ken, the rooms are arranged in the following sequence (Fig. 129): a wooden-floored

93. Shoi-ken teahouse seen from outside the villa. Katsura Imperial Villa.

kitchen with a sunken hearth, and a seven-and-a-half-mat, a six-mat, and a four-mat room. The whole complex conveys a rural, rather than a *shoin*, style. But in the design of each room we discover the painstaking attention paid to fine details. For example, in the Ni-no-ma (Naka-no-ma), the wall below the window is lined with velvet in the bright Ichimatsu checkerboard pattern, cut off obliquely at the bottom (Figs. 94, 95); in the *kokabe* (transom-like wall) facing the pond there are six large round *shitaji-mado* (Fig. 82); and the *fusuma* of each room have door pulls cleverly shaped like oars (Fig. 159). The simple design of the shelves in the wooden-floored kitchen and the pantry (Fig. 97) shows such sensitivity that these shelves seem to belong to the best of teahouse equipment.

Careful attention to such details makes it clear that, though the Shoi-ken borrows its external appearance from the farmhouse, its design undeniably echoes both the refined tastes of the nobility, as with the Shokin-tei, and the sensitivities inherent in the austere teahouse tradition.

MINOR STRUCTURES. Among other structures in the Katsura garden, there are two small resthouses, the Shoka-tei and the Manji-tei, and one small Buddhist hall, the Enrin-do. The Shoka-tei, also called the Tatsuta-ya, is situated atop the hill between the Shokin-tei and the Shoi-ken. It is a small tea hut where visitors rested during their garden tour, appreciating cherry blossoms in spring and maple trees in autumn. The Manji-tei, located behind the Shokin-tei, in the most sequestered area

94. *Window and velvet wall decoration, Ni-no-ma, Shoi-ken teahouse. Katsura Imperial Villa.*

of the garden, also served as a place to rest while strolling through the wooded park. These two structures are nothing more than very simple roofed benches, but they were designed with consummate skill, as is evident in the Shoka-tei. The precisely balanced composition of each of the windows in the Shoka-tei (Figs. 18, 96) and the four benches of the Manji-tei (Fig. 154), each of a different size and with a different form of railing, exemplify the designers' artistry. The alertness and sensitivity of the designers are particularly apparent in small-scale architecture. The Enrin-do is a memorial hall, where the mortuary tablets of Hosokawa Yusai and the Hachijo prince of each generation are enshrined. Though built in the temple style with a tiled roof, the Enrin-do is carefully located so as not to disrupt the harmony of the surrounding landscape.

THE NEW SHOIN. In Prince Noritada's last years and even shortly after his death, the retired emperor Gomizuno-o paid several visits to Katsura. For such occasions it seems that a considerable number of alterations were made in the garden and the buildings. Most affected among the buildings was the New Shoin. Its architecture, both in atmosphere and in minute detail, befits the brilliance of an imperial suite.

The large hipped-and-gabled roof rises powerfully, and along two sides of the complex runs a veranda, one *ken* (about six feet) wide, enclosed by wooden storm shutters. The overall feeling is quite different from that of the Old and the Middle *shoin,*

95. *Detail of Ichimatsu-pattern velvet wall decoration, Ni-no-ma, Shoi-ken teahouse. Katsura Imperial Villa.*

which, with their exposed verandas, are more informal in design; instead, a palatial dignity has been added here. The expression is similar in feeling to that of the imperial structures at Nijo Castle, the Kyoto residence of the Tokugawas.

In the New Shoin an eight-mat and a six-mat room and a three-mat area are arranged in an L shape next to the tatami-floored section of the veranda. The three-mat section, which is the innermost area, is the *jodan* (raised-floor section), or the seat of honor. It is further defined by a coffered ceiling overhead and by a *tsukeshoin*, an alcove containing a large window with a broad sill about one-third of a meter above the floor. The famous Katsuradana (Katsura Shelves; Fig. 9) are in the corner opposite the entrance. Adjacent to these

rooms are the imperial bedchamber, the consort's dressing room, a pantry (Fig. 81), a wardrobe, a bath, a toilet, and a washroom (Fig. 118). These accommodations were presumably for the retired emperor's use. In these rooms too a variety of tasteful shelves were installed, among them the famous Ura Katsuradana in the dressing room (Fig. 98) and in the imperial bedchamber the triangular cabinet called the Gyokendana, or Shelf for the Imperial Sword (Fig. 119).

It has long been pointed out that the New Shoin is designed with a sensitivity quite unlike that of the Old and the Middle *shoin*. For example, bark is carefully left on the edges of the decorative beam above the lintels, and the nailheads in this beam are covered with splendid daffodil-shaped caps

(Fig. 156). In the eight-mat room a motif taken from the Chinese character for "moon" is used for the *fusuma* door pulls (Fig. 115). The area around the *jodan* is particularly decorative; the coffered ceiling is made of zelkova wood, and the Katsura-dana, of rare imported wood.

The view of the garden from the New Shoin is no less impressive than that of the interior of the building. The part of the garden extending from the New Shoin to the Shoi-ken consists of a flat, moss-dotted lawn, believed to have been used as a court for *kemari* (an ancient form of football in which the contestants tried to keep a deerskin ball in the air by kicking it) and for archery, of which Prince Noritada was very fond. Under the eaves, where the lawn comes up to the building, there is a bed of gravel and tiles, a neat linear composition. Thus the garden area bordering the New Shoin imparts a clear, crisp feeling, unlike that induced by the sturdy and rugged steppingstones lined up in front of the Old Shoin or the austere rock arrangement in the tea garden extending up to the Shokin-tei.

At Katsura villa, a wide variety of buildings is dispersed amid the scenic beauty of ponds, streams, islands, shoals, bridges, hills, bamboo groves, and other visual delights. We wend our way from one to another of these buildings by footpaths of steppingstones or by boat. The garden serves as a backdrop for the architecture; seen from the buildings during moon and snow viewing, receptions,

97. *Tea-utensil shelves in pantry, Shoi-ken teahouse. Katsura Imperial Villa.*

◁ 96. Shitaji-mado *of Shoka-tei teahouse. Katsura Imperial Villa.*

and other entertainments, the man-made scenery sets the theme for the architecture.

Imagine the scene when Prince Toshihito and the retired emperor Gomizuno-o came here for relaxation: music and poetry recitations in the *shoin* or in the Shokin-tei and *kemari* on the lawn at midday; moon viewing on the *shoin* veranda or at the Geppa-ro from dusk till late evening; and morning tea receptions in the Shokin-tei at dawn. Depending on the season, at the Shoi-ken or the Shoka-tei there must have been drinking fests combined with maple or snow viewing and firefly chasing. Pastimes suitable to the individual character of each season unfolded in succession. In the context of these varied activities, it is impossible to describe Katsura simply as a monument to archi-

98. *Ura Katsuradana shelf arrangement, Dressing Room, New Shoin. Katsura Imperial Villa.*

99. *Interior of New Shoin, showing enclosed* ▷ *veranda and Jodan-no-ma. Katsura Imperial Villa.*

tecture or garden art or by any other isolated attribute. The Katsura villa is indeed a synthesis of architecture and landscaping that graces a land known since ancient times to have been blessed with bountiful natural beauty.

What then are the outstanding characteristics of Katsura? Preeminent must be the total integration of landscape and architecture. The placement of such architectural accomplishments as the Old and the Middle *shoin*, the various teahouses, and the New Shoin is restrained with remarkable skill. But these structures do not follow a uniform pattern; they are not works unified by a single theme or style. Rather, each of them expresses its distinct individuality. The simple yet powerful spatial composition of the Old and the Middle *shoin*, the

resplendent *shoin* rooms and the serene *wabi* (rusticly simple) tearoom juxtaposed in the Shokin-tei, and the domestic *minka* style of the Shoi-ken exemplify the individual qualities of theme and expression inherent in each structure. These diverse manifestations are integral components of this well-organized architectural work.

In architectural classification, Katsura villa falls into the style known as the *sukiya zukuri*, or teahouse style. This style emerged when the austere *soan* style of teahouses, which had been created in the Momoyama period by such great tea masters as Sen no Rikyu (1520–91), was incorporated into the contemporary residential style; that is, the *shoin zukuri*. It deviates significantly from the formality-laden brilliance of the halls of Nijo Castle. With

its flexible room arrangement and such materials of natural feeling as clay walls, *shitaji-mado,* and bark-covered posts and decorative beams, the new style better suits the taste of the Japanese. For this reason, from the Edo period (1603–1868) down to the present, nearly all Japanese domestic architecture has followed this style.

Katsura villa is one of the earliest examples of *sukiya zukuri,* or *shoin zukuri* that incorporates elements of tea architecture. There is great variety in the design of the structures; the Old and Middle *shoin* faithfully adhere to the rules of the *shoin* style, while the Shoi-ken and the Geppa-ro emphasize the subtleties of the *sukiya* style. Unlike the case of the *sukiya*-style buildings of the mid-Edo period and later, there was no prototype that Katsura could have followed. Rather, it exhibits complete creative freedom. Indeed, Katsura was an expression born when the *sukiya* style itself was born.

The second of Katsura's eminent characteristics is the perfectly balanced sense of design that strikes one's eye throughout the garden and architecture. We find this everywhere, from the exterior of the Old Shoin and the interior of the Shokin-tei to the steppingstones and paving. To be sure, each element was conceived as an integral part of the theme and design of the landscape or structure to which it belongs; but at the same time, all are individual works of creative art offering ample latitude for appreciation. It is this vivid expression of each element that contributes to the richness of the overall design.

CHAPTER FOUR

The Designers

THE QUESTIONS OF who actually conceived the plans for such great monuments as Nikko and Katsura and how these undertakings were organized are intriguing. Inasmuch as these works are not random assemblages of simple styles but have elaborately structured layouts and architecture, we must assume the existence of strong leaders to supervise the projects, in addition to the artisans who actually carried out the construction. Here we shall devote our attention to the prime movers, the leaders involved in these projects: Kora Munehiro at the Tosho-gu, Heinouchi Masakatsu at the Taiyu-in, and Princes Toshihito and Noritada at Katsura.

KORA MUNEHIRO   As was mentioned earlier, the 1634–36 construction of the Tosho-gu was directed by Kora Munehiro, Titular Governor of Bungo and a master builder for the shogunate. He headed a huge corps from the "first drawing of the adze" (the opening ceremony) through the "raising of the ridgepole" (completion of the framework). As grand paymaster, Munehiro put his seal to the general account book *Tosho-gu Gozoei-cho,* acknowledging payments to the workmen. Moreover, in an assortment of documents he is mentioned as the general supervisor of the Tosho-gu construction.

Kora Munehiro was originally a craftsman in the village of Kora, Omi Province (present-day Kora-cho, Inukami-gun, Shiga Prefecture). The famous two-story gatehouse built in 1566 at the Aburabi

Shrine in this district is an early extant work by his family. Excellent shrine construction was the hallmark of Omi craftsmen in the late middle ages, or the fifteenth and sixteenth centuries; and among craft families, Munehiro's was one of the most illustrious.

According to records handed down in the Kora family, Munehiro began serving the Tokugawa clan at Fushimi, in southern Kyoto, in 1596. His reputation grew after he worked in Kyoto on the Yoshida Shrine and some structures in the Konoe residence. In 1604 he went to Edo and in the following year participated in the work on Zojo-ji temple and, it is recorded, on the Hommaru (main) compound of Edo Castle. But on consulting more accurate sources we find that Munehiro actually rose in the ranks of shogunal carpenters somewhat later, in the late 1620s. Besides the Nikko Tosho-gu, representative extant works by Munehiro include Tokyo's Taitoku-in Mausoleum (erected in 1632 but largely destroyed during World War II) and the five-story pagoda (1639) at the Kan'ei-ji, also in Tokyo. In 1636, the year that saw the completion of his greatest achievement, the Tosho-gu, Munehiro, at sixty-two, relinquished his post to his son and successor Munetsugu. Returning to Kora, he lived out his remaining years in seclusion. A portrait sculpture of him (Fig. 100), said to have been carved by Munehiro himself, is maintained in his family temple in Kora.

Research in various historical sources to uncover

100. *Detail of* Portrait of Kora Munehiro. *Colors on wood; height, 43.6 cm. Yuinen-ji, Shiga Prefecture.*

101. *Detail of* Portrait of Prince Hachijo Toshihito. *Manju-in, Kyoto.*

the exact role Munehiro played in the Tosho-gu construction reveals that rather than being simply a carpentry foreman he was more an architect: his supervisory powers and authority were extremely far-reaching.

First, in terms of stylistic choice, the most basic of architectural decisions, we can see his versatility in the ingenious contrasts attempted in the Tosho-gu's secondary structures. The work on the Front Gate and the Middle Treasury indicates a sure knowledge of classical architecture. Such work could have been conceived only by a master architect with both long years of training and familiarity with a variety of styles. The architectural plans of the Tosho-gu are not extant, but the plan for a miniature shrine to be used in the Taitoku-in Mausoleum, which bears the signature and seal of Munehiro, has been found in the Kora family archives. While directing his team, Munehiro must have labored long over drawing such plans to design the overall structure of the Tosho-gu complex.

Second, Munehiro was apparently an expert sculptor, a necessary qualification for any architect of high repute in the Momoyama period. Even if he himself did not carve the many sculptures at the Tosho-gu, they must certainly have passed his inspection for final decisions on style and theme. It appears that at the Tosho-gu he also originated a new concept of compound architecture, combining varied styles. From the numerous proposals recorded in the confidential instructions handed

102. *Interior of main sanctuary, showing miniature shrine. 1632 (destroyed in World War II). Taitoku-in, Tokyo.*

down in the Kora family we can see that the artisans of the time were quite excited about the innovative layout of the planned buildings.

Munehiro's success in using his talents to the full, as evidenced by the Tosho-gu, was made possible by the remarkable technical progress in the field of architectural design on the one hand and by the adoption of a bureaucratic system in the construction department of the shogunate on the other.

TECHNICAL PROGRESS. Sometime during the transition from the Momoyama to the Edo period, plans, cost estimates, bids, and construction began to be made on the basis of large-scale architectural plans. Until the middle ages, drawings for construction included only simple floor plans. Elevations and plans of details had never been drawn in advance, and decisions on the dimensions of structural parts depended heavily on experience or else had

to be made as the construction progressed. However, at the end of the middle ages elevations came into use. This advance is closely connected with the nearly concurrent development of *kiwari jutsu,* or the art of determining construction ratios, as a means of regulating dimensions and proportions of structural elements. (The Japanese module is based on interpost spans, thickness of posts, and width of rafters.) It was due primarily to the refinement of *kiwari jutsu* that architectural design employing complete plans began to be implemented.

Kiwari jutsu was highly refined in the Momoyama period, and a number of fairly systemized manuals on the subject were written. One of the most important of these is the *Shomei,* an extant work prepared in 1608 by Heinouchi Yoshimasa and his son Masanobu. The *Shomei* consists of five volumes, each dealing with a single subject: palaces and

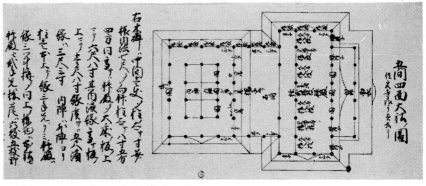

103. *Two pages from* Shomei, *by Heinouchi Yoshimasa and Heinouchi Masanobu. 1608. University of Tokyo.*

residences, gates, shrines, temples, and towers. In each volume, detailed information is given for structures of different styles and scales. The *kiwari* techniques, most of which were kept secret, were quietly passed down from master to pupil by renowned carpenters of the day, such as Kora Munehiro.

Most *kiwari* manuals are organized so as first to illustrate the overall layout and ground plans of the various structures in mansions, temples, and shrines, then to give precise information on the design of specific structures. Some of the ground plans incorporated ideas previously unknown in Japan. In a sense, *kiwari* manuals served as architectural encyclopedias in which all the existing technology of Japanese architecture was assembled and presented in a systematic form.

BUREAUCRATIC SYSTEM. In tandem with technical progress in design arises the question of how to organize the artisans. The most notable change in the status of craftsmen was the result of the establishment of an organized system in the construction department of the shogunate. As early as the Muromachi period (1336–1568) the post of commissioner for construction had been established within the administrative hierarchy and workers were assigned to his service, but the number of paid workmen was small. In the Momoyama period a considerable number of workers were retained by daimyo, or feudal lords, in order to construct castles and battlefield fortifications; but the system of retaining carpenters was very loose knit in comparison with the bureaucratic organization of later times. It was only around the turn of the seventeenth century that artisans' organizations began to take form, but by the 1630s they had been accorded

104. Main Hall of Futarasan Shrine. 1619. Nikko.

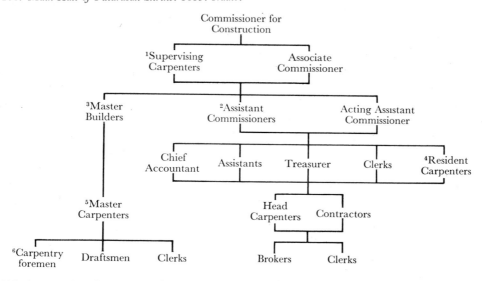

105. Organization of construction department of Tokugawa shogunate. The numbers indicate the relative ranks of the carpenters. Adapted from Yasu Tanabe, "On the System of the Construction Department in the Edo Shogunate," Journal of Architecture and Building Science, *no. 598 (1935), Architectural Institute of Japan.*

106. *Balustrade and log-cabin-style wall of Middle Treasury. Nikko Tosho-gu.*

official status in the carpentry departments of the shogunal and local governments.

From about 1590 onward, the artisans attached to the shogunate operated in two groups, under the direction of the Suzuki and Kihara families. These groups were engaged in the construction of the castle and other buildings in Edo. For the construction of shrines and temples in the Edo environs sponsored by the shogunate around 1620, a Suzuki and a Kihara served as superintendents; their assistants included the heads of the Tanida, Fukami, and Sugimoto families, among others. Working under these assistants were a number of head carpenters assigned to specific duties. By this time roles and organization in the construction department had become fairly clearly defined.

In 1632 the post of commissioner for construction became a permanent office, and the bureaucratic structure of the construction department was officially established. Figure 105 indicates roughly how the department was organized. Both administrative officers, such as the commissioners and the accountants, and technical officers, such as the master builders and the foremen, were included. Those directly involved in overseeing the carpenters were the supervising carpenters, assistant commissioners, master builders, resident carpenters, master carpenters, and carpentry foremen, ranking in that order. These posts were hereditary and were controlled by just a few families. For example, in the early Edo period, supervising carpenters came from the Suzuki, Kihara, Nakai, and Katayama fami-

107. Left to right: *Washbasin Shed, bronze torii gateway, and Sutra Repository. Nikko Tosho-gu.*

lies; assistant commissioners were from the Kata-yama, Naito, Tanida, Hayashi, Yoshimoto, and Sugimoto families; and master builders were from the Kora, Heinouchi, Tsujiuchi, Tsuru, and Benkei families. The Nakai and Benkei families were based in Kyoto and were involved in the work on the Kyoto Imperial Palace, Nijo Castle, and other projects in the Kinai (Kyoto-Osaka-Nara) area. As their annual stipend, the Nakai received 1,000 *koku* (about 5,000 bushels) of rice; the Kihara, 750 *koku* (3,750 bushels); and the Katayama, Kora, and Heinouchi, 100 *koku* (500 bushels) each. These annuities were roughly equivalent to those accorded to samurai of medium and low standing in the military hierarchy.

Among the artisans of the construction depart-ment, the responsibility for architectural design rested on the shoulders of master builders. The Kora being the inheritors of the closely guarded *kiwari jutsu* teaching of the Kenninji school, and the Heinouchi and the Tsuru that of the Shitennoji school, these families became famous as temple and shrine designers. These men all came from the Kan-sai area, a locale known since the middle ages for its superior architectural heritage. (The Kora and the Tsujiuchi were from Omi, or present-day Shiga Prefecture, and the Heinouchi and the Tsuru from Kii, or present-day Wakayama Prefecture.) In contrast, most of the supervising carpenters and assistant commissioners were from eastern prov-inces, such as Totomi (in present-day Shizuoka Prefecture), Suruga (also in present-day Shizuoka

108, 109. Korean lion-dog guardians sculpted by Heinouchi Masanobu. Colors on wood; height of lion-dog at left, 76 cm.; height of lion-dog at right, 78 cm. 1619. Kashima Shrine, Ibaraki Prefecture.

Prefecture), and Musashi (present-day Tokyo and Saitama Prefecture).

Roughly during the period between the Battle of Sekigahara (1600)—when Tokugawa Ieyasu's Eastern Army defeated Toyotomi Hideyoshi's vassals' Western Army—and the Winter and Summer Sieges of Osaka Castle (1614–15), the rising military class and the construction it sponsored in the Kanto area attracted these artisans from Kansai. Among the Tokugawa-affiliated artisans who had established hegemony over Edo's organized carpenters, these men who migrated from western Japan gradually came to the fore and through their excellent design skill finally became master builders. Reliable records indicate that their elevation to master builders did not occur until well into

the late 1620s. Perhaps the Taitoku-in Mausoleum (1632) by Kora Munehiro and Heinouchi Masanobu, and the Tosho-gu (1636) by Munehiro can be considered testimony that they had indeed secured their positions. Inscriptions bearing Munehiro's name left inside the Kan'ei-ji five-story pagoda (1639) attest also to his authorship of this magnificent temple, whose construction was begun in 1626.

In this historical context, it becomes clear that the 1634–36 construction of the Tosho-gu coincided with the acme of technical and organizational progress in the early Edo period. This is further evidenced in the architecture of the Tosho-gu itself. Both the large-scale ground plan that encompassed and unified various styles and the liberal adoption

110. Detail of juncture of Main Hall and Ai-no-ma. Taiyu-in.

of new techniques seen in the stonework and stone walls testify to the integration of contemporary architectural developments. The generous use of gold in ornamentation and of bronze sheets in fireproof roofing owed much to great advances made in mining, which also illustrates a technological growth that contributed to the advancement of Edo architecture.

HEINOUCHI
MASAKATSU
The post of general supervisor for construction of the Taiyu-in Mausoleum was occupied by Heinouchi Masakatsu, Titular Governor of Osumi (in present-day Kagoshima Prefecture) and head of the Heinouchi family, who together with the Kora held the position of master builders in the shogunal department of construction. The family originally came from Negoro, in what is now Wakayama Prefecture. Among the earliest works of this family are the main hall and two-story gatehouse of the Wakanoura Temman-gu shrine (1606), by Masakatsu's grandfather Yoshimasa. Apparently Yoshimasa served the Toyotomi clan: he was one of the head carpenters in the construction of the Kyoto temple Hoko-ji and of the Hokoku Mausoleum. His son Masanobu, however, transferred the loyalties of the family to the Tokugawa shogunate, and together with the Kora advanced to the peak of the contemporary architectural world, thereby ensuring the future of the Heinouchi family. Masanobu's principal achievement was the Taitoku-in Mausoleum; the Lotus Hall (about 1620) of the Rinno-ji

111. *Boathouse. Katsura Imperial Villa.*

temple in Nikko is also attributed to him. This is the illustrious father whom Masakatsu succeeded as master builder.

The fact that the Taiyu-in is the work of a master builder who was fully as able as Kora Munehiro is interesting enough, but equally interesting is the fact that Masakatsu was a second-generation master builder. Unlike his father and Munehiro, whose architectural genius was nurtured by the ambitious spirit of the Momoyama period and who made their way to the top of their trade through ferocious competition, Masakatsu had simply inherited his family's position. The Tosho-gu and the Taiyu-in are separated by fewer than twenty years; but as we have seen, there is an appreciable difference in design. This dissimilarity may be attributable to an aesthetic discrepancy stemming from the generation gap.

THE HACHIJO PRINCES The design of Katsura differs considerably from that of Nikko.

Tradition has it that the excellent architecture and landscaping at Katsura originated with Prince Toshihito himself. According to another tradition, they were designed under the direction of the famous aesthete Kobori Enshu (1579–1647). In any case, the names of the carpenters, masons, and sculptors have not been handed down as they have been for Nikko. But besides Princes Toshihito and Noritada, who were the patrons, it is obvious that there were many other people connected with the construction, such

112. Stone bridge viewed from Ni-no-ma, Shokin-tei teahouse. Katsura Imperial Villa.

113. Bamboo hedge known as Sasa-gaki surrounding villa grounds. Katsura Imperial Villa. ▷

as consultants, field supervisors, carpenters, gardeners, masons, and other artisans.

The two princes' diaries and other records make it very clear that both were knowledgeable in the fields of architecture and landscaping. Prince Toshihito's diary makes frequent mention of building a teahouse at his main residence, of transplanting in the gardens, and of rearranging garden stones. From his manifest interest in garden design and tea architecture, we may assume that he actually participated in directing the work. Prince Noritada, who inherited his father's enthusiasms, went to Sakai, near Osaka, to study Sen no Rikyu's teahouse; and while taking a cure at the hot springs of Arima, in what is now Kobe, he took time to select some rocks to be used as steppingstones in his garden.

Prince Noritada's strong attachment to Katsura and concern with its construction are revealed in letters from Josho-in (d. 1661), his mother, and from Ume-no-miya (1620–48), his younger sister. They make references to Toshihito's frequent visits to the construction site during the years around 1645. (The *Josho-in Shosoku* and *Ume-no-miya Shosoku,* the collections of the two ladies' correspondence, are now housed in the Imperial Household Agency, Tokyo.)

One letter in the *Josho-in Shosoku* collection says: "How delighted I was with the tea gathering yesterday, using new tea leaves! Everything is so charming, and the teahouse in particular has come along marvelously. You have planned so long for this work, and the result is exactly as you wished. I congratulate you on its success."

A letter in the *Ume-no-miya Shosoku* collection says: "Is the teahouse going to be the same as before? I'm sure the construction will be reminding you of the past."

From these passages alone it is difficult to determine whether the structures referred to here are actually those of Katsura; but in all likelihood they are, since on the advice of his friends, the sickly prince frequently visited Katsura to recuperate. It is therefore reasonable to suggest that the second phase of Katsura's construction took place under Prince Noritada's watchful eye.

Now we should turn our attention to the people who guided the planning and supervised the actual work on the garden and the buildings. Traditionally, Kobori Enshu has been regarded as *the* man responsible. Recently, however, more and more scholars seem to agree with the theory postulated by Osamu Mori, director of the Garden Culture Research Institute, in his *Katsura Rikyu* (1955) that the major roles were actually played by Nakanuma Sakyo in the time of Prince Toshihito and by Ogawa Bojo Shunsho in the time of Prince Noritada. Nakanuma Sakyo (fl. c. 1600) was both the elder brother of the well-known tea master and calligrapher Shokado Shojo (1584–1639) and a distant relative of Kobori Enshu. Sakyo was an attendant at the Ichijo-in, a branch temple of the Kofuku-ji in Nara. He made frequent visits to the noble Konoe family and was evidently very active in Kyoto social circles. Dr. Mori identifies this Sakyo with the close friend of Prince Toshihito who appears by the names Shunan-in and Sakyo in the prince's diary and elsewhere. However, as Hide-

114. *Interior of Hasso no Seki tearoom. 1628. Konchi-in, Nanzen-ji, Kyoto.*

haru Hisatsune, a leading authority on Japanese garden art, points out, there are certain factors that make it difficult to accept this hypothesis; and we must say that the connection, if any, of Nakanuma Sakyo, as well as of Ogawa Bojo Shunsho, with the construction of Katsura has not been established.

The real name of Kobori Enshu was Kobori Masakazu. Because he was Titular Governor of Totomi (in present-day Shizuoka Prefecture), he was commonly known as Enshu, an abbreviated form of "province of Totomi." The legend that Enshu designed Katsura was first recorded in mid-Edo-period chronicles; but records from the time of construction fail to corroborate this story, and its validity is questionable. Enshu established a name for himself in the Kyoto area as the shogunate's

commissioner for work on the Kyoto Imperial Palace, Sento Imperial Villa, and Nijo and Osaka castles. He was the ideal man to seek advice from regarding the design of the Katsura villa or to commission as supervisor of the actual construction work. Moreover, Enshu was the most influential tea master of the day: he was the tea instructor to Shogun Iemitsu. Among the Kyoto nobility, most followers of the cult of tea fell under his sway; and Prince Toshihito relied heavily on Enshu for the manufacture and selection of tea utensils. In the architecture of Katsura, too, there are a number of elements that are recognizably in Enshu's style. For example, as was noted earlier, the Shokin-tei teahouse has many features in common with the Hasso no Seki of the Konchi-in (Fig. 114). However, we cannot generalize from this fact and as-

115. Door pull patterned after the Chinese character for "moon" used on fusuma between Ichi-no-ma and Ni-no-ma, New Shoin. Katsura Imperial Villa.

116. Decorative door pull used on cryptomeria door, New Shoin. Katsura Imperial Villa.

sume that Enshu had anything to do with other parts of the villa.

Whether or not Kobori Enshu actually directed the construction of the Katsura villa at the request of Prince Toshihito is still open to debate. But in recognition of Enshu's prowess in architecture and the cult of tea it is safe to assert that the villa's design was to a great extent influenced by his style.

The names of other craftsmen involved in the villa's construction are unknown, as we have mentioned. The only name of which we are certain is that of the painter Kano Tan'yu. Seals reading "Tan'yu" appear on the ink paintings on the miniature *fusuma* of the Katsuradana and Ura Katsuradana in the New Shoin. In December 1638, when he took the tonsure, Kano Morinobu changed his art name from Uneme to Tan'yu, so the shelves

could not have been built earlier than that date.

The many gaps in our knowledge of how the construction of Katsura villa was organized remain unbridged, but there is no question that the roles played by Princes Toshihito and Noritada themselves were of pivotal importance to the decisions made concerning the plan and design of the villa. This is not only because they were conversant with architecture and landscape gardening but also because the people involved in the construction felt very strongly that the greater part of the accomplishments at Katsura emanated from the princes' insights. In the previously quoted opening lines of the *Keitei-ki,* for example, we saw praise of Prince Toshihito's gentlemanly character and excellent abilities; and in the *Nigiwai-so,* a tea book by Haiya Shoeki (1611–91), who was a tea master and con-

fidant of Noritada's, that prince's relationship with Katsura is described as follows:

"Around the Kan'ei era [1624–44] there was a noble prince by the name of Hachijo-no-miya Noritada. He was so gentle in both appearance and disposition that he seemed to be of superhuman origin. . . .

"Later, on recovery from an illness, he frequented a place in western Kyoto called Katsura, where the previous lord [Toshihito] had built a simple teahouse. The prince ordered it to be furnished and had his craftsmen construct several buildings and hillocks, lay out steppingstones, and divert waters from the Katsura River. . . .

"To the newly completed villa he invited those tea masters whose names were trumpeted about the land and prepared tea for them. He did so with such dexterity that all marveled at his inventiveness and wondered: 'Is there anyone like him in all the world?' "

Perhaps such praise as "inventiveness" and "exactly as you wished" voiced by his contemporaries is inflated by affection and reverence; nonetheless, these words are evidence that the plan of the villa evolved through the prince's proficiency in architecture and landscaping.

MEN OF CULTURE   The principal engineers in
VERSUS ARTISANS   the creation of Katsura villa
were the Hachijo princes, both highly cultured gentlemen. In contrast, in the construction of Nikko, the chief architects, Kora

117. *Detail of crawl space beneath the veranda of the New Shoin. Katsura Imperial Villa.*

118. *Interior of washroom, New Shoin; notice stand for bucket in center. Katsura Imperial Villa.*

Munehiro and Heinouchi Masakatsu, were artisans. The difference in character and background of the central figures in these two projects is crucial to a comparison of the design of the two works.

Among the administrators of the Nikko project, the foremost man among the educated intellectuals was Tenkai, a high priest of the Tendai sect of Buddhism, who had a comprehensive knowledge of Shinto and Confucianism. He was the principal advocate of adopting for Ieyasu's enshrinement the formalities of Sanno Ichijitsu Shinto (Hie Shinto), a faith closely connected with the Tendai sect. Tenkai personally supervised the two-part ceremony called *nawabari* (rope stretching), which is performed before construction begins. In the first half of the ceremony, the sacred territories of the precinct are separated from the profane with ropes; and in the second, the layout of structures and walls is indicated, again with ropes. That he played a central role in the Nikko project is reflected in his letters from around 1630, which tell us that he was so busy that he was unable to leave Nikko. Even so, we cannot infer that Tenkai exercised a decisive influence on determining the actual design of the buildings. Other extant works constructed under Tenkai's supervision—such as the Nikko Tosho-gu's subsidiary shrines in other prefectures, which also bear the name Tosho-gu—present thoroughly different stylistic features; and he does not seem to have had much interest in architectural design.

The inspiration for Prince Toshihito's direction of artisans and laborers to produce a unified design

that satisfied him must have derived from the way Sen no Rikyu oversaw the designing of his teahouses and gardens. Before Rikyu, there were some champions of architecture and landscape gardening who devoted themselves to the actual work—certain Heian nobles when constructing their palatial residences, and the eighth Ashikaga shogun, Yoshimasa (1435–90), when building his Eastern Hills Villa in Kyoto—but Rikyu was the first to be conscious of his role as an artist. It was reported that he always carried a measuring stick and constantly reviewed the dimensions of the rooms and inspected the arrangements of tea utensils as he surveyed the work. His was the path to architectural creation shaped by the heightened sensitivities of a tea man, a course markedly different from the

eminently practical approach of the artisan. At Katsura, too, the fact that Prince Toshihito took an active role in creating the design does not imply that he maintained surveillance over technical matters. However, it is apparent that both his knowledge of cultural tradition and his keen sensitivities developed by the cult of tea were applied down to the smallest detail in the designing of the Katsura villa.

A comparison of the construction at Katsura and Nikko invites the question whether or not their builders actually came from completely different social environments. The startling contrast in expression in these two monuments tends to lead an observer to infer that they were built by totally unrelated groups of people. However, a close rela-

119. *Gyokendana, or Shelf for the Imperial Sword, in Imperial Bedchamber, New Shoin. Katsura Imperial Villa.*

120. *Sculpted Chinese lion on end of bracket arm supporting veranda of Yomei-mon gate. Nikko Tosho-gu.*

tionship between their builders did actually exist.

Kano Tan'yu, for example, not only supervised painting the buildings at the Tosho-gu and the Taiyu-in but also executed the *fusuma* paintings of the Katsuradana. His younger brother Naonobu (1607–50), who reputedly worked on the *fusuma* paintings in the Katsura Middle Shoin and Shoi-ken, was also one of the shogunate painters at Nikko. Suden, the abbot of the Konchi-in, who contributed equally with Tenkai to founding the Tosho-gu, composed the *Keitei-ki* at Katsura in honor of Prince Toshihito.

Kobori Enshu, at the very time that he is believed to have exercised great influence on the Katsura construction, was one of the closest aides to Shogun Iemitsu. At the time of the Nikko com-

pletion ceremony in 1636, which was to be performed in Iemitsu's presence, Enshu was advancing his career as magistrate of Fushimi and as commissioner for landscape gardening at the Sento Imperial Villa in Kyoto. He was specifically summoned by the shogunate and entrusted to inspect the preparations being made at Nikko for the shogun's pilgrimage. We do not know the exact nature of Enshu's mission, but it is probable that he acted as an adviser to Iemitsu on the shogun's inspection tour on the Tosho-gu's completion.

As we have already seen, Kora Munehiro, from Omi Province, was quite active in the architectural world of Kyoto. According to his family records, in 1596 he erected a gate for the Konoe, a family of imperial advisers, and was rewarded with

121. Decorative beams and sculpture on wall of Ishi-no-ma. Nikko Tosho-gu.

the title Lieutenant of the Palace Guards. Konoe Nobuhiro (d. 1649), a nephew of Toshihito's, often visited Katsura at the prince's invitation, and the prince participated frequently in tea gatherings held at the Konoe residence. Therefore, if the Kora family records are accurate, in his youth Munehiro apparently worked very closely with the Hachijo family.

Such evidence indicates that the builders of Katsura and Nikko were not unrelated at all; on the contrary, it is essential to recognize the deep bond among them in order to consider their lives and times. Of course, in designing Nikko, Kora Munehiro did not duplicate the style that he had em-

ployed at Kyoto in his youth. He had to go to Edo in search of work and fight a long, fierce battle to attain the rank of master builder. Only then was it possible to address himself to the challenge of creating a totally new architectural style in the rugged natural setting of Nikko.

The rich, forceful beauty and expression seen at the Tosho-gu are not directly representative of the architecture of Kyoto, but are deeply rooted in the harsh climate and firm tradition of the Kanto region. At the same time, the Tosho-gu is a product of the vigorous spirit of the people who had flocked to the burgeoning young capital of Edo in search of a new life and freedom.

CHAPTER FIVE

A Dual Tradition

**COMMON CHARAC-
TERISTICS: SYNTHESIS
AND FREEDOM** Both Nikko and Katsura inherited the legacies of many architectural traditions. Foremost among them were the resplendent temple and shrine styles that flourished in the Momoyama period and the *soan* (thatched hut) style of teahouse established by such tea masters as Sen no Rikyu.

Precursors to the Nikko Tosho-gu style include the Kara-mon (Chinese-style gate) at the Daitoku-ji in Kyoto and the Kara-mon of the Hogon-ji in Shiga Prefecture—works encrusted with bold sculpture and, in the manner of Toyotomi Hideyoshi's Juraku-dai castle-palace, presenting a magnificent, heroic appearance. At Nikko there are also numerous details taken from the styles of ancient Buddhist temples and of medieval Zen monasteries.

The atmosphere at Katsura is created by the free use of natural materials and a keen compositional sense. This natural effect originated in the teahouses of the Momoyama period, such as Rikyu's Tai-an in the Myoki-an temple, Kyoto, and the Jo-an in Aichi Prefecture by Nobunaga's younger brother Oda Urakusai (d. 1621), who studied under Rikyu. Katsura also owes its style to the residential architecture of both the aristocracy and the commoners and to ancient and medieval garden art combined with the later garden art associated with the tea ceremony.

Thus we see that, while one is based on the temple and shrine style and the other on the teahouse style, the architecture at both Nikko and Katsura is an assemblage of a variety of styles developed prior to the Edo period. The new styles generated in the Momoyama period acquired broader contexts of expression when combined with styles that had dominated the mainstream of Japanese architecture in earlier times. Painted and sculpted ornaments adorning gates, halls, and shrines were now evaluated in terms of how they related to the overall ground plan in the compound; the compact and pleasing design of the ceremonial tearoom was invigorated when integrated into spacious living quarters or teahouses.

What was attempted in the massive accumulation of styles at Nikko and Katsura was not merely the juxtaposition of different architectural idioms but the realization of a fresh and unified design for a shrine compound in one case and for landscape gardening in the other. Here was a spirit of experiment, a synthesis of styles. Thus both works are outstanding examples of the transition from the bold and imaginative products of the Momoyama to the vast monuments of the Edo period.

Another characteristic of early Edo architecture is the unrestrained freedom in design seen at both Katsura and Nikko. This freedom signals the zenith of an architectural power quite distinct from that represented by the castles and teahouses of Momoyama times. Taken individually, the Katsura and Nikko structures may be no match for Momoyama

122. Kara-mon gate reputedly moved to present site from Hokoku Mausoleum (present-day Toyokuni Shrine), Kyoto. Early seventeenth century. Hogon-ji, Shiga Prefecture.

123. Interior of Jo-an teahouse. Circa 1617. Inuyama Hotel, Inuyama, Aichi Prefecture.

124. *Eaves bracketing and decoration of Main Hall. Nikko Tosho-gu.*

works in terms of originality or striking expression; but in the grand-scale Edo works one theme after another unfolds as in a panorama, displaying design variations born of unbridled fantasy.

The variations from the elegance of the latticed-windowed wall to the elaborate ornamentation of the Kara-mon and further to the animated, variegated beauty of the Main Hall at Nikko, and the changes in interior design from the Old Shoin to the Shokin-tei and further to the Shoi-ken at Katsura demonstrate that the imaginative powers and abundant architectural creativity of the period were in no danger of withering away. This freedom of design indeed makes Katsura and Nikko stand out distinctly from both their predecessors and their successors.

We have already noted that the expressive force of the ebullient sculpture at the Tosho-gu had, in the Taiyu-in twenty years later, become a neater but more enervated form. At Katsura, too, the spatial tensions that we encounter in the Old Shoin and the Shokin-tei have been replaced in the New Shoin by merely amusing decoration. It should be remembered that the temples, shrines, castles, and teahouses before the time of Katsura and Tosho-gu had been built according to austere, sharply defined principles: for example, in one of Rikyu's ceremonial tearooms we find serious thought and severity rather than extravagance or variety.

In synthesis of styles and freedom of design, Katsura and Tosho-gu are unparalleled. However, there are weaknesses and contradictions in both, for

example, the careless grouping of subordinate buildings at the Tosho-gu and the overzealous use of *shitaji-mado* and stone lanterns at Katsura. But in such extensive architectural creations, one must never allow minor infelicities and errors to overshadow the fine overall qualities. Rather, we should direct our attention to the strength of an age that was filled with boundless energy and that possessed the capacity to give concrete form to that energy. From the beginning we have stressed the fundamental differences of environment, objective, and expression between Katsura and Nikko; but in terms of synthesis and freedom in design—accomplishments that these greatly contrasting works share—we must recognize the true breadth of architectural creation.

DIVERSE CONDITIONS Aware of the above circumstances, we can now return to the question of how two diametrically opposed architectural styles were arrived at for Katsura and Nikko. The contrast cannot be ascribed simply to the difference in function or in the people for whom they were intended, that is, imperial courtiers and shogunal delegates. We must examine the relation of the architectural styles to the climates of their sites and to the mentality of the designers.

We noted a sharp contrast in the ways the sites for these two projects were selected. On the one hand, Katsura was intended to take advantage of the cultural ambiance of Kyoto, a world deeply rooted in the elegant traditions of the Heian court

◁ 125. View of inner courtyard; left to right: Yomei-mon gate, Shin'yo-sha (Portable-Shrine Storehouse), and Kara-mon gate. Nikko Tosho-gu.

126. Detail of stone wall beside Front Gate. Nikko Tosho-gu.

as represented by the poetry anthology *Kokin Waka-shu* and the romantic novel *Genji Monogatari*. On the other hand, Nikko with its severe Kanto climate was a land that had nurtured indigenous folk beliefs, and the site for the Tosho-gu was selected on the basis of political rather than aesthetic considerations. In short, Katsura was based on the traditional splendor of the imperial court, and Nikko on the frontier spirit.

The builders who determined the overall design also occupied contrasting positions. The fact that the central figures at Katsura were the Hachijo princes, both highly cultured connoisseurs, and at Nikko were Kora Munehiro and Heinouchi Masakatsu, both hereditary artisans, made a crucial difference in even the most fundamental aspects of architectural planning and methods. For the craftsman, architecture consists of styles pertaining to details, techniques employed in framing the structure, actual carving of sculpture, and so on—that is, areas where he can visibly display his prowess. In contrast, the gentleman is interested in the overall expression of sensitivity and taste rather than in technical particulars. When these factors are taken into consideration, it becomes apparent that to view Katsura only as a culture-oriented manifestation of court architecture and Nikko only as a political product of the shogunate is an oversimplification, acknowledging only the immediate social implications.

It is obvious, as we have noted, that neither of these complexes was built by men acting in isola-

127. *Stone lantern known as Sanko Lantern by boat landing in front of Shoi-ken teahouse. Katsura Imperial Villa.*

tion. We have seen that Kobori Enshu and Kora Munehiro actually had close ties to both projects. Nor did their contemporaries have such a limited perspective as to consider the two works as products of two completely unrelated worlds.

In support of this assertion, let us consider two structures of the Konchi-in subtemple of the Kyoto Zen temple Nanzen-ji: the Tosho-gu and the Hasso no Seki. The Konchi-in Tosho-gu has wooden members that are lacquered black and vermilion and decorated with colorful patterns, imitating Nikko in style as well as in name. The Hasso no Seki (Fig. 114) is an excellent example of a *soan*-style teahouse, very similar to Katsura's Shokin-tei. Both buildings of the Konchi-in were erected in 1627 by Suden, then abbot of the Nanzen-ji, prob-

ably in anticipation of the shogun Iemitsu's visit to Kyoto. The construction of both was supervised by Kobori Enshu, and in Suden's diary we read: "For the shrine [Konchi-in Tosho-gu], the *kusari-no-ma* [room for informal tea], and the *sukiya* [tearoom], Enshu's style will be the most appropriate. I ordered him to make sure that everything will be done accordingly." The design style bearing Enshu's stamp must have included much of the Konchi-in, including the Tosho-gu, the teahouse, and the garden, for one can see how the silhouette of the Tosho-gu is skillfully blended into the background of the famous dry-landscape garden called the Crane and Turtle Garden, whose stone arrangements symbolize those auspicious animals.

The Konchi-in provides a convincing argument

128. Shoka-tei teahouse viewed from veranda beside Gakki-no-ma. Katsura Imperial Villa.

against concluding that Katsura and Nikko were built by people unconnected with each other. Rather than adopt a restricted viewpoint in comparing Katsura and Nikko, it is wise to recall once again that Japanese architecture produced almost simultaneously two vast monuments with enormously contrasting characters, and that both works fully express the vigor of the age.

A DUAL TRADITION   In reviewing the processes of creating Katsura and Nikko, we encountered two viewpoints: one emphasizing the traditional virtues and the other embodying a fresh frontier spirit; or to put it in another way, the viewpoints of the gentleman and of the artisan. These are the two threads that run

through the fabric of the history of Japanese architecture.

The Fujiwara architectural aesthetic of Heian times was directly based on the refined tastes and sensitivities of the nobility. For example, in the Byodo-in temple, founded in 1052 by the imperial adviser Fujiwara Yorimichi (992–1074) at the site of his father's villa in Uji near Kyoto, the overall appearance of the famous Ho-o-do (1053), or Phoenix Hall, is indeed graceful. Its interior is so richly adorned as to lead believers to feel that they are in the Pure Land, the paradise of Amida Buddha. However, the style of its ornamental details and technical improvements lacks creativity, and consequently the hall does not signify a great advancement in terms of structural composition. In contrast,

129. *Interior of Shoi-ken teahouse. Katsura Imperial Villa.*

in Kamakura-period architecture, the artisans who worked in the *tenjiku-yo* (Indian style) and the *kara-yo* (Chinese style) concentrated on framework and bracketing, making structural details their primary sphere of activity. The great reconstruction of the Todai-ji, the "Great East Temple" of Nara, sponsored by the military dictator Minamoto Yoritomo (1147–99), would have been an impossibility for the refined cultural tastes of the Fujiwara nobility. The *tenjiku-yo*, which later became known as the *dai-butsu-yo* (Great Buddha style), suited the reconstruction at the Todai-ji, and new architectural techniques and vigorous craftsmanship produced a fresh expression.

We can also see a dual architectural tradition in the development of castles and teahouses during the Momoyama period, the age preceding that of Katsura and Nikko. Japanese castle architecture, typified by the donjon and subsidiary turrets, originated in warlords' fortified mansions and was furthered by the development of fireproofing techniques that included use of stone fences and plastered clay walls. The aim was practical, purely for defense, and little attention was paid to the traditionally esteemed qualities of grace and elegance. But the addition of structural and technical innovations created a previously unseen quality of architectural aesthetics. In contrast, in the *soan* style of teahouse, developed by Sen no Rikyu, there is a strong attachment to the traditional values of *wabi* (rusticity), *sabi* (austerity), and *yugen* (mysterious grace), which had outlived the Heian

130. Door pull shaped like pine needles used on fusuma *in Gakki-no-ma. Katsura Imperial Villa.*

poetry and Muromachi aristocracy that gave them life. The thatched roof adapted from peasant architecture, the unplastered clay walls, the *shitaji-mado,* and the bark-covered posts—in other words, elements that emphasized simplicity and natural beauty—were selected according to the strict aesthetic standards of the cultured gentleman, not according to the conventions of the artisan, who was responsible only for the actual work.

In any account of the tradition of architectural design or of the architect's profession in Japan, one must consider not one single lineage but the dual heritage of the gentleman and the artisan. Within this broad perspective of Japanese architectural creation, we should evaluate Katsura and Nikko not in order to elevate either the gentleman or the artisan at the expense of the other, but on the basis of their achievements, each firmly rooted in its own tradition, in visualizing and accomplishing a great synthesis on a scale without precedent.

Katsura's refined sensitivities perpetuating the elegance of the imperial court and Nikko's spirited conquering of a new environment and fierce natural conditions, together with the keen aesthetic eye of the Katsura gentlemen and the explicit technical endeavors of the Nikko artisans, are a legacy of such importance that nothing can be isolated or discarded. If we are to learn anything from these two works, we must embrace a perspective broad enough to encompass the whole of this varied tradition.

CHAPTER SIX

—·—

Commentaries on Major Illustrations

HIGHLIGHTS OF KATSURA AND NIKKO FIGURE 7. The Katsura Imperial Villa is situated on one bank of the Katsura River, quiety tucked away amid a jumble of rice fields about two and a half miles west of Kyoto Station. Visitors number fewer than two hundred daily, and one might walk along the bamboo outer fence in an attempt to make a full circle only to find himself ending up in a nearby farmer's garden or lost among the field paths in the little village of Shimo Katsura. When the villa was built here, the area was one of the more thriving of Kyoto's suburbs; and a highway leading to western Japan through the adjacent provinces of Tamba and Settsu passed nearby. Now National Route 9 has taken its place.

The land area of the villa is about sixteen acres; and on the east, toward the river, is a large dike. The present height of the dike is due to fairly recent construction; but long ago a pine grove extended along the bank, and from part of the villa one could look over the embankment and watch people on the other side fishing for river trout. Frequently Prince Toshihito would cross this river by boat on his visits to the villa. In bygone days, the little village of Senshoji across the river was the Hachijo family estate, and the river fishing and the ferry trade came under the family's control. Because the villa faced the clear river, being able to watch pleasure boats on the river and to drink in the surrounding natural beauty were among the greatest attractions of life in the villa.

On the boundary of the villa compound facing the river, living bamboo have been bent and woven together to form a hedge, the Sasagaki. On the north side, on either side of the Front Gate slender bamboo twigs have been wedged in among thicker upright bamboo stems to form the Katsuragaki (Fig. 1). In other places a simple bamboo fence separates the compound from the neighboring fields. These types of fences, which have been employed by peasants in Kyoto's suburbs for centuries, help the villa's rustic exterior to blend unobtrusively with the fields and the river, creating a rapport between the villa and its unspoiled surroundings.

Formal entry to the villa is made through the Front Gate and the Miyuki-mon; then walking along the Miyuki-michi, and passing through the Inner Gate, one finally arrives at the Mikoshi-yose (Palanquin Approach) on the north side of the Old Shoin. This is quite a long walk, but it is very refreshing: the path, covered with fine bluestone, passes through thatched gates and crosses over earthen bridges before reaching the Old Shoin. The path from the Miyuki-mon is lined with hedges and maple trees; and the name Miyuki-michi, or Imperial Path, suggests that the lane was laid out

131. *Bamboo hedge known as Sasagaki and dike alongside Katsura River. Kyoto.*

132. *Sasagaki hedge seen from inside the villa, showing how living bamboo is woven into the fence. Katsura Imperial Villa.*

for the visits of the retired emperor Gomizuno-o.

The Mikoshi-yose, the formal entrance hall to the Old Shoin, is where members of the imperial family long ago got into and out of the palanquins that carried them to and from town. Usually, even a simple entrance to a *shoin* has a broad platform and a door decorated with many rails as indications of formality. But here, at Katsura, all expressions of formality have been eliminated, leaving only a simple porch and wooden door. It is because of this simplicity that our impressions of the Mikoshi-yose are indelible.

A straight walkway of closely laid stones stretches from the Inner Gate to the Mikoshi-yose. To the right of the pavement, looking toward the veranda of the former kitchen, several steppingstones are scattered, and to the left a few others are placed in the direction of the small gate leading to the Geppa-ro. Just in front of the Mikoshi-yose porch there is a big stone step, known as the *kutsu-nugi ishi,* or "shoe-removing stone." The design of the stone walkway and this stone step has been praised as "Enshu's orthodox steppingstones and the step for six." "Orthodox" here meant exactitude or rigid adherence to formality—a concept compared

to the formal block style of calligraphy. "Six" apparently refers to the size of the rock, large enough for six people to leave their footgear on. The walkway is worthy of the name Imperial Path; it has the finest, most indomitable quality of all the stone arrangements in the villa. The dignity of the formal entryway, the Mikoshi-yose and the stone walkway, is expressed not by lavishness or spaciousness but by simple, clear-cut linear shapes. Here is the epitome of the basic theme of the villa's design.

FIGURE 8. Staggered in a zigzag pattern by the pond in the center of the compound lies a large *shoin* cluster, facing roughly to the southeast. From right to left, the cluster consists of the Old Shoin, the Middle Shoin, the Gakki-no-ma, and the New Shoin. The densely thatched roofs seem to crisscross, and the stark white of the shoji alternating with the dark wooden doors recedes into the shadows of the cluster. Together, roofs, doors, and shoji enhance the subtle, delicate beauty of the whole structure. Used also in Nijo Castle, the zigzag layout pattern—or the "files of flying wild geese," as the Japanese call it—originated in residential architecture in the *shoin* style. It is a radical departure from the *shinden* style of Heian times, in which the

133. *Commoners' houses in Shimo Katsura area built along former highway. Kyoto.*

eaves of buildings connected with corridors all met at neat right angles. One purpose of the zigzag pattern is to link smoothly the suites of *shoin* rooms that are arranged in an L shape; the diversity of garden views afforded by this layout is a handsome bonus.

Another feature contributing to the beauty of the *shoin* complex is the raised-floor style of construction. The facts that the area was close to a river and subject to periodic flooding and that the ground was continually damp dictated the use of this method of construction; however, in compensating for these conditions, a spark of originality produced an airy design. The Old Shoin stands relatively high off the ground, and its crawl space is enclosed with a plastered wall. In the Middle and the New *shoin* the wall of the crawl space is set back from the edge of the verandas, which project beyond the core structure. The bamboo-grate vents inset here and there in the crawl-space walls add a nice accent.

The wooden doors and the shoji along the sides of the Old Shoin are installed in an ancient style, with two doors and one shoji set into each bay. In the New Shoin, shoji and the wooden doors that shield them from rain run the entire length of the building. In the Middle Shoin, originally, doors like the ones in the Old Shoin were placed three feet in from the lip of the veranda and the veranda was exposed to rain; but now the veranda has rain doors along its outside edge.

In the *shoin* complex the raised-floor construction and the old-style wooden doors were introduced for practical reasons, and the zigzag floor plan is the result of multiple construction; but the end product is the achievement of superb composition.

FIGURE 9. In the New Shoin, in one corner of the *jodan*, or section with an elevated floor, there is an L-shaped cluster of display shelves known as the Katsuradana. Along with the Kasumidana in the teahouse at the Shugaku-in Villa and the Daigo-

134. Miyuki-mon (Imperial Gate). Katsura Imperial Villa.

135. Mikoshi-yose (Palanquin Approach) and stone-paved walkway. Katsura Imperial Villa.

dana in the Sambo-in at the Daigo-ji, the Katsura-dana has been praised as one of the three best shelf arrangements in Japan. This set of shelves is considered to be representative of Enshu's "orthodox" style.

As we see in Figure 9, several cabinets, some with wooden doors and others with *fusuma,* are skillfully joined to heighten the effect of straight lines. Rare imported woods, such as rosewood, ebony, ironwood, and betel palm, enhance the shelves with a variety of colors and textures. The landscapes and figures painted on the *fusuma* are identified from the seals as the work of Kano Tan'yu.

With the arched black-lacquered frame above the *tsukeshoin* window to the left of the shelves and with the coffered zelkova-wood ceiling, the *jodan* is perhaps the most exquisite, skillfully decorated part of the villa. The color scheme of the room is primarily black and white, with various neutral tints added for accent, completely avoiding strong

colors. Circles and arcs are artfully distributed throughout the larger composition of intersecting straight lines. With its clean lines and light feeling, the decoration of the *jodan* is vastly different from that of the Kara-mon (Fig. 10) at the Tosho-gu.

On the posts flanking the shelves and on the center board of the *tsukeshoin* window there are cuts and deep scratches that have been filled. Perhaps this damage was suffered during installation or later alterations. It is presumed that sometime after the New Shoin was completed the *jodan* was rapidly remodeled to its present appearance. If this is the case, it would support the view that the *jodan* fixtures were later additions in preparation for the visits of the retired emperor Gomizuno-o.

In the New Shoin, such outer rooms as the *jodan* and the Ni-no-ma, which has door pulls shaped like the Chinese character for moon, exhibit a rather lively design. However, the inner rooms, such as the Dressing Room and the Pantry (Fig. 81), have a plain yet attractive design. Whether

136. The cryptomeria-lined Nikko Highway, which connects Nikko and Tokyo.

as if symbolizing the severe natural scenery. In this plain setting, the elaborate white, gold, red, blue, and green decoration of the Kara-mon assaults the eye.

At left in Figure 10 is the latticework set into the side of the Kara-mon. The design is a type of floral relief worked into a pattern of large intersecting circles. The floral motifs are painted alternately in blue and green, and since other parts of the design are painted in vermilion and gold, the effect of the colors changes according to the viewer's position and the direction of the light. Perhaps a stained-glass window offers the best Western comparison to the effect of this openwork panel. At right in Figure 10 is one of the paneled doors of the Kara-mon. Inlaid in the middle panel is a plum carving of rare imported wood. Peony and chrysanthemum ornaments have been applied to the lower panel.

Comparing the decoration of the Kara-mon with that of the Katsuradana, we see that though they are contemporaneous and have some features in common, such as the use of imported wood, the overall feeling is utterly dissimilar. In contrast to the clear geometric composition of circles and straight lines in the Katsuradana, the Kara-mon features a complexity of intersecting circles and knotlike frets. In color scheme, bold hues like gold, red, and blue are used in the Kara-mon, in opposition to the neutral tints at Katsura. If we were to select two characteristics of the decoration at the Tosho-gu, they would be this intertwining of straight and curved lines and the color scheme full of gold and vivid primary colors.

FIGURE 11. This illustration shows the juncture of the Ishi-no-ma and the Main Hall. At right is the side wall of the Ishi-no-ma; at left is the Main Hall; and in the center, at the end of the balcony, is a swinging door. On the back of this door is a magnificent *maki-e* painting of plums and chrysanthemums.

In terms of both architectural technique and decoration, the connection of the Ishi-no-ma and the Main Hall is the showpiece of its creators. In the older style of *gongen zukuri*, such as employed here, the roof of the *ishi-no-ma* cuts directly into the structure of the main hall, creating a gap between

this variation was intended from the planning stage or resulted during later revision is a question calling for further research.

FIGURE 10. Today Nikko is an easily accessible tourist attraction; the Tosho-gu precincts are inundated by throngs of tourists every summer. In the old days, however, because of its location at the extreme northern edge of the Kanto area, the sacred precincts could be reached from Edo only by an arduous journey of at least four days. As today, the natural surroundings were severe: the climate was cold and the mountainous area was buried in forests of towering cryptomeria. It is a refreshing surprise to visit Nikko in midwinter: not a soul in sight, only the buildings contrasting sharply with the snow-cloaked earth. In the spectacular Tosho-gu compound, the steppingstones and shrubs and mosses of Katsura are completely gone; the precincts are covered simply with gravel,

the heights of the two, which is then closed with boards. In the newer style, the *ishi-no-ma* eaves are curved upward to join those of the main hall. This newer style is what we find at the Taiyu-in (Fig. 36); however, the creators of the Tosho-gu were unaware of this technique.

With the boldly curved beam joining the two structures and with the carvings of peonies and Chinese lions, the wall decoration of this section perhaps constitutes the Tosho-gu's most powerful expression. This strength is enhanced by the extraordinary look both of the *baku* carved in the bracketing of the Main Hall and of the dragons under the corner eaves.

Bell-shaped, ogee-arched windows (called *kato-mado*) with embossed grillwork patterns are set into the walls of both the Main Hall and the Ishi-no-ma. In both windows the *hanabishi* (flower diamond) pattern is incorporated into the *tatewaku* (undulating-line motif), a pattern still seen in kimono design. The color scheme of these windows is the same as that of the side panels of the Kara-mon. The coloring is most effective when the windows are viewed from inside the Ishi-no-ma.

FIGURE 12. On the far side of the Tamagaki, the latticed-windowed wall, we see on the right the roof of the Worship Hall and on the left the roof of the Main Hall, with its forked finial and ridge billets perched atop the soaring roof. The roofs are now covered with bronze sheets but were originally roofed with cypress bark, probably giving a more venerable general appearance.

On the upper and lower *nageshi*, or decorative beams, of the latticed-windowed wall, there is a continuous tortoise-shell pattern painted in lead-oxide pigments mixed with a special vegetable oil that gives the paint a lustrous quality. Between the beams are elliptical windows whose lattices are decorated floral reliefs like those in the Kara-mon. In the Tamagaki latticework, gold leaf is applied to the frets; the interior surfaces are painted vermilion, and the flower petals are painted in blue and green. As one walks past the wall, the shimmering color pattern flickers continually, the elusive red appearing, disappearing, and reappearing. This effective decoration greatly enhances the Ta-

137. *Five-story pagoda and, just visible at left, stone torii gateway. Nikko Tosho-gu.*

magaki, which is seen to best advantage as one walks slowly alongside it. The transoms of the Tamagaki are decorated with large intricate sculptures of waterfowl and flowers, each carved from a single piece of wood.

The Tamagaki wall joins both sides of the Kara-mon, and the floral reliefs on the side panels of the gate, shown in Figure 10, are an uninterrupted extension of the line of the wall. On the façade of the Kara-mon primary colors are not used; we find only white and brown. But on the sides there is a full range of colors. The bright color scheme on the sides of the gate is not fully consistent with the decorative plan of the Kara-mon; but the bright colors are necessary to a smooth blending of the colors of wall and gate.

In decorating the Tosho-gu, attention is paid not only to expressive effects in individual structures but also to the effects of contrast and smooth transition, in addition to the effects of color variation seen while walking, such as in the Tamagaki wall.

FIGURE 13. Painted on the large arched beam of the Washbasin Shed are peonies, arabesque patterns, and dragon medallions. Below the beam are swirling waves, and above the beam are dragons flying above waves. On beam surfaces and other visible structural members at the Tosho-gu, one often sees painted patterns with medallions scattered across them. The Front Gate tie beams, for example, have a continuous pattern of flower diamonds on which Chinese lions in circles are superimposed. The patterns themselves are known as *oki-mon* (recipient pattern), while the lions and dragons withing the circles are called *hon-e* (real pictures), that is, individually painted pictures, not stenciled forms. This type of design is also used on the front tie beam of the Middle Treasury (Fig. 48), on the pillars of the Yomei-mon, and elsewhere in the precincts.

A design painted on a pattern raised with layers of whitewash, as in the case of the beam in Figure 13, is called *okiage-zaishiki* (embossed coloring), while a design painted directly on a wooden surface is called *hira-zaishiki* (flat coloring). Compared with flat coloring, the bas-relief-style embossed coloring requires an incredible amount of time and effort to execute effectively, and it is not often seen in architecture of that time. Most of the Tosho-gu shrines in other areas employ only flat coloring. Even in the Nikko Tosho-gu, the coloring of minor buildings like the Okari-den (temporary sanctuary) is in the flat style; only the principal structures within the Front Gate are accorded the time-consuming bas-relief embossed coloring.

As we see in Figure 52, at each of the four corners of the Washbasin Shed there are three stone pillars. The pillars all appear to be vertical; however, careful measurement reveals that they lean slightly inward at the top. In later washbasin sheds, such as the one at the Taiyu-in, the departure from the vertical is more pronounced. Modern shrines built throughout the country also follow the new style. With the Tosho-gu pillars the degree of inclination from the vertical equals only ten percent of the width of the pillars. This minute departure

from the vertical is another indication of the antiquity of the shed. The barely perceptible slant of the pillars, which imparts a certain stability to the lines of the structure, is further evidence of the great care that the builders lavished on their creation.

NIKKO: CHINESE AND JAPANESE STYLES

FIGURES 26 AND 27. The architectural style employed in the Yomei-mon is a nearly pure form of the *kara-yo,* but with a considerable amount of sculpture added. The *kara-yo*—literally, "Chinese style"—was imported from China, along with Zen Buddhism, during the Kamakura period and was used in such Zen temples as the Engaku-ji and Kencho-ji in Kamakura. The reliquary hall at the Engaku-ji is recognized as an example of the purest form of the *kara-yo.* Gradually, this architectural style began to appear in Buddhist architecture outside the Zen sect. In the early Edo period, the *kara-yo* was frequently used in architecture of the Nichiren and Jodo (Pure Land) sects. The front gate of the Jodo-sect temple Zojo-ji in Tokyo, built slightly earlier than the Tosho-gu, exemplifies the adoption of the *kara-yo* by other Buddhist sects.

The main characteristics of the *kara-yo* are:

1. The use of round pillars with tapered capitals. The pillars rest on multiple plinths shaped very much like the beads of an abacus.

2. Above the pillars, the arms of the elaborate bracketing complex, which supports the roof or a shallow balcony, fan out in all directions—to both sides, as well as to front and back. As shown clearly in Figure 26, brackets are used not only directly above the structural columns but also above the intercolumnar spans. (In the *wa-yo,* or Japanese style, the bracket arms extend only to the front and back, not to the sides; and brackets are used only directly above the pillars.) The arc of the elbows of the bracket arms is circular, in contrast to the nearly elliptical arc of the elbows of *wa-yo* bracket arms.

3. Radial raftering, called fan-rib raftering, is used. In contrast, *wa-yo* rafters are all parallel to each other.

4. The unusual caps on the newel posts are

138 (right). Okiage-zaishiki (embossed coloration) used in exterior of Gokuro. Nikko Tosho-gu.

139 (far right). Floral openwork pattern incorporated in latticed-windowed wall. Nikko Tosho-gu.

140 (right). Metal fittings on nageshi *beam decorating latticed-windowed wall. Nikko Tosho-gu.*

141 (far right). Fretwork combining hanabishi *(flower diamond) and* tatewaku *(undulating lines) motifs, Shin'yo-sha (Portable-Shrine Storehouse). Nikko Tosho-gu.*

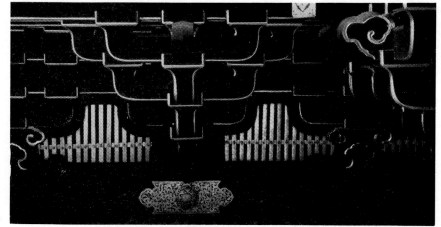

142. Detail of bracketing supporting veranda of Ai-no-ma showing gilt edges of bracket arms. Taiyu-in.

shaped like inverted lotus blossoms, while *wa-yo* newel-post caps are onion shaped.

5. Instead of lap-jointed tie beams, tenoned tie beams are used to connect the through-mortised pillars, greatly reinforcing the structural framework. Among the crossmembers is a type called the shrimp beam because of its strongly curved shape.

6. Instead of rectangular windows, the *katomado* is used.

7. The doors are not made simply of single slabs of wood but are paneled, divided by mullions and rails.

As one can see in Figure 26, the Yomei-mon is faithful to the *kara-yo* style, as is reflected in the plinths and tapered capitals of the pillars, in the radial raftering, and in the decoration on the newel posts.

The sculptural motifs just under the eaves of the Yomei-mon include dragons on the bracket ends, entwined dragons on the uppermost tie beam, dragon-horses (dragons with single-toed hoofs) on the ends of the lower tie beam, dragons under the hip rafters, unicorns within the Chinese gables (under the arched eaves), and phoenixes on the panels between brackets. Fanciful Chinese lions adorn both the uppermost tie beam and the first tier of bracketing, supporting the shallow balcony. Exotic animals and rare birds are the dominant decorative motifs; however, the frieze between the rails of the balcony balustrade depicts Chinese children at play, and between the brackets supporting the balcony are sculptures depicting events in the lives of famous Chinese sages. The only traditional Japanese motifs used are the openwork carvings of peonies on the panels of the open bays where the two guardian deities are seated and the large relief peonies on the panels at the sides of the open bays. It is obvious that a great effort was made to create a Chinese atmosphere in and around the Yomei-mon.

Shown in Figure 27 is perhaps the most spectacular sight at the Tosho-gu: the highly sculpted panels that embellish the outer wall of the corridor on either side of the Yomei-mon. Extended along their high stone foundations, these corridors can truly be called galleries in the artistic sense. Never

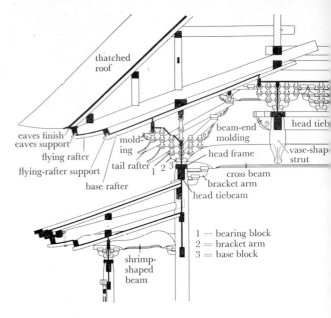

before the Tosho-gu had such bold expression been achieved, although a similar effect was attempted in ornamental carving during the Momoyama period, as exemplified by the frieze around the veranda of the abbot's residence at the Zuigan-ji in Matsushima, Miyagi Prefecture. A bronze sconce, presented by the Dutch government, is attached to the wall beneath each of the fifty sculpted panels. During the Edo period, on the eve of a festival, when the shrine palanquin was moved to the point from which the ceremonial procession would start on the following day, all the candles in the sconces and stone lanterns were lighted. One can imagine that in the flickering candlelight the sight of the sculpture floating eerily in the darkness must have been breathtaking.

FIGURES 28 AND 29. In the courtyard beyond the Yomei-mon there are three buildings: the Shin'yo-sha, the Kagura-den, and the Shrine Office. These buildings are artistically arranged as focal points of the courtyard. The *o-mikoshi*, the portable shrines that are used during religious festivals, are stored in the Shin'yo-sha. Sacred music and dance are

◁ *143. Sectional view of Reliquary, Engaku-ji, Kamakura, Kanagawa Prefecture, exemplifying* kara-yo *construction.*

145. Detail of Jizo Hall, Shofuku-ji, Tokyo, showing typical kara-yo *bracketing.*

144. Detail of five-story pagoda, Daigo-ji, Kyoto, showing typical wa-yo *bracketing.*

performed in the Kagura-den; and in the Shrine Office (former Homa Hall) the *goma* (Sanskrit, *homa*), an esoteric Buddhist purificatory fire ritual, is performed. These three buildings are uniform in size, each being a square three bays wide and three bays deep. The Shrine Office, however, has an extended roof at the rear.

In sharp contrast to the Yomei-mon, the Kagura-den is built almost entirely in the *wa-yo* style. *Wa-yo*, it will be recalled, is the architectural style that was popular in Japan before the introduction of the *kara-yo* during the Kamakura period. Exemplars of the *wa-yo* style are the Itsukushima Shrine at Miyajima, Hiroshima Prefecture, and the Byodo-in at Uji, south of Kyoto. In reality, the *wa-yo* is also a Chinese style; but it was brought to Japan very early during the Asuka period (552–646). Because it is so much older than the *kara-yo* and is so firmly entrenched in Japanese architectural tradition, the *wa-yo* is thought of as the "Japanese style."

The distinctive features of the *wa-yo* are: 1) the pillars have neither plinths nor rounded capitals; 2) the bracketing does not fan out to the sides; 3)

the rafters are set parallel; 4) brackets are used only directly above the pillars, and various types of struts, including the frog-crotch strut, are used above the intercolumnar spans; and 5) decorative half beams are often used on the outer surface of tie beams.

The styles of the structural framework and balustrades in the *wa-yo* also differ from those in the *kara-yo*. Compared to the *kara-yo*, with its elaborate structure and opulent decoration, the *wa-yo* is relatively simple and uncluttered.

The bracketing, frog-crotch struts, and balustrades of the Kagura-den are all in the *wa-yo* style. In addition, some elements borrowed from the residential style are incorporated, such as the *shitomi-do* (latticed doors hinged at the top), square pillars, and unusually extended eaves. Bird-and-flower motifs and arabesque patterns are used in the painting and sculpture, and there is not the slightest hint of the Chinese subject matter found in the Yomei-mon. To summarize, through both decoration and architectural style, the Kagura-den transmits an elegant Japanese atmosphere, in total

146. Kagura-den (Sacred Dancing Stage). Nikko Tosho-gu.

147 (opposite page, left). Shrine Office (former Homa Hall). Nikko Tosho-gu. ▷

148 (opposite page, right). Shin'yo-sha (Portable-Shrine Storehouse). Nikko Tosho-gu. ▷

contrast to the definite Chinese air of the Yomei-mon.

The Shin'yo-sha and the Shrine Office are still different in feeling. The somber, even solemn, color scheme of the Shrine Office, with black predominating, differs markedly from the lively coloring of the Kagura-den. The Shrine Office uses *kara-yo* bracketing, but the Shin'yo-sha bracketing is *wa-yo*. However, the Shin'yo-sha windows are the bell-shaped *katomado* of the *kara-yo*, and its transom carving is far more elaborate than that of the Kagura-den.

The differences among these three buildings extend even to the roofs. The Kagura-den has a simple hipped-and-gabled roof (Fig. 146); the Shin'yo-sha has a Chinese gable or *karahafu* added to its hipped-and-gabled roof (Fig. 148); and the Shrine Office has a small portico extending from its hipped-and-gabled roof (Fig. 147).

Comparing these three structures, we see that the Shrine Office is most consistently in the *kara-yo* style and that the Kagura-den adheres most rigidly to the *wa-yo*. In the Shin'yo-sha, the two styles are skillfully integrated. For example, in the Shin'yo-sha balustrade the *wa-yo* onion-shaped newel-post caps coexist with the *kara-yo* lotus-shaped struts and the "bracken sprout" bend that finishes the top

rail (Fig. 148). The *karahafu* gable, *katomado*, and the plain board ceiling used here are details normally found in the *kara-yo* buildings at the Tosho-gu. The pillars of the Shin'yo-sha are square and their edges are beveled and grooved, which clearly shows a strong *wa-yo* influence. Because of this melding of styles, the Shin'yo-sha has a definite baroque flavor. Moreover, in terms of sculpture and the patterns painted on some of its members, this building is the most striking and elaborate of the three.

The stylistic contrasts and variations among these three buildings isolated in the courtyard between the Yomei-mon and the Kara-mon demonstrate the careful planning that was so crucial to the overall design of the Tosho-gu.

FIGURES 30–32. The pillars, beams, and gables of the Kara-mon are brilliantly whitewashed, as are the jambs, lintels, and panels of the doors of this gate. Furthermore, the chrysanthemum moldings on the ends of the tie beam tenons, the transom frieze depicting the legendary Chinese emperor-sage Shun's reception of courtiers, and the high-relief sculptures of iris and such marsh plants as arrowhead on the beam above the transom frieze are also whitewashed. Exotic imported woods in their natural colors are used for the inlaid bas-relief sculptures: the dragons that climb up and down

150 · COMMENTARIES

the pillars and door jambs; the plum blossoms, peonies, and chrysanthemums that bloom on the door panels; the plums that blossom on small panels between the rails and mullions of the doors; the cranes that are scattered across the tortoise-shell pattern on the tie beam within the gable; and the dragons that flourish on the bargeboards. After white and natural wood colors, the most prominent color in this gate is the gold of all the fittings, although vermilion is used liberally on brackets and the undersides of beams and touches of blue, green, and black appear on the almost-hidden rafters. But even with the use of other colors, the Kara-mon gives the impression of a regally stark white gate.

A look at the underside of the eaves (Fig. 32) reveals bursts of gold design inlaid in vermilion- and black-lacquered grounds, as well as green, blue, and vermilion on a gold ground. The extent of the artists' skill is apparent in this decorative color combination, which almost seems to vibrate with a life of its own. As we saw in Figure 10, these rich colors are repeated in the stunning fretwork panels set into the sides of this gate.

The bronze animals perched on the ridgecourses are the work of Shiina Hyogo, the foremost bronze caster for the shogunate when the Tosho-gu was constructed. Atop the front gable is a beast-god

who, according to Chinese legend, is the guardian of the night; and on the gable on either side is the forked-tailed dragon who is the guardian of the day.

FIGURES 33–36. One distinctive feature of the architecture at the Tosho-gu is the abundant use of gold leaf in decoration. At both the Tosho-gu and the Taiyu-in, gold leaf has been lavished on the Main Hall, perhaps to emphasize its status as the most important structure within the compound. However, the way gold leaf is employed is quite different in these two shrines. The various methods of using decorative gold leaf (illustrated in Figures 33 and 34) can be reduced to a few categories:

1. Gilt metalwork. This includes the decorative metal fittings on the ends of the veranda planks, the newel-post caps, the nail covers on the decorative beams, the rafter ends, the eaves tiles, the bargeboards, and the so-called gold brocade below the capitals of the structural pillars. The base metal for the fittings is copper about two or three millimeters thick and is worked with engraved or *repoussé* patterns of grass scrolls, goldthreads, hollyhocks, and so forth. The surface of the design was lacquered and gold leaf was then pressed into the still-moist lacquer. In another technique, the base metal was plated with gold amalgam. Finally the design was highlighted with India ink.

2. Gilt lacquerwork. This method of applying gold leaf over several layers of lacquer is used in decorating the lintel and in the backgrounds of the panel paintings shown in Figure 33.

3. Gilt trim. This refers to the gilt lacquer applied to the beveled edges of such members as the bracket arms and bearing blocks supporting the roof.

4. Gold inlay. Gold was inlaid in incised designs, such as the arabesque patterns on the bracket arms.

5. *Maki-e* (lacquerwork with embedded gold dust or particles). We have already noted a limited use of this technique in the Kara-mon; however, *maki-e* is used generously in the arabesque design on the rails of the paneled door seen at right in Figure 33. Unfortunately, in this illustration we cannot see the inner sanctuary of the Main Hall, where artists employed perhaps the highest refinements of *maki-e*, such as the technique of embedding chips of gold foil in the lacquer and the so-called pear-skin technique, in which gold dust is sprinkled on the surface of the work before the final layer of lacquer is applied.

6. *Ike-zaishiki* (coloring). This technique, seen in the Washbasin Shed decoration in Figure 13, is simply painting colors directly on gilt-lacquered sculpture. Examples of *ike-zaishiki* in Figures 33 and 34 are the chrysanthemums between the bracketing supporting the veranda, the peonies on the paneled doors, the chrysanthemums in the transom, and the dragonlike beasts, phoenixes, and chrysanthemums in the gables.

7. *Goku-saishiki* (brilliant coloring). This is the technique of applying gold leaf to the standing portions of relief patterns that have been painted. As shown in Figure 34, this technique has been used in the gable on the tortoise-shell pattern on the lower tie beam and on the linked-diamond pattern on the upper tie beam.

At the Tosho-gu the use of gold leaf is limited to decorative ornamentation and patterns. It is rare to see gold applied to such structural members as pillars and beams, which are either whitewashed or lacquered black or vermilion. At the Taiyu-in, however, the situation is quite different. As can be seen in Figure 35, pillars and other structural members are completely gilded; and wall panels are lacquered black, in contrast to the gilt lacquerwork at the Tosho-gu.

Thus, although both the Tosho-gu and the Taiyu-in at first seem to be drenched in gold, there is a manifest difference in the manner and degree of use. The lavish use of gold leaf at the Taiyu-in perhaps represents the origin of the copious use of gold so widespread in Buddhist architecture from the mid-Edo period onward.

Figures 37 and 38. Architectural sculpture, such as is seen in these two figures, was not carved by professional sculptors but entirely by ordinary carpenters at the time the Tosho-gu was built. In those days there were sculptors and engravers who specialized in Buddhist images; at the Tosho-gu these artisans worked only on such free-standing works as the statues of the Nio (Benevolent Kings) in the Front Gate, the guardian deities in the Yomei-mon, and the lion-dog guardians.

Of the two groups of sculptors who executed the Tosho-gu sculpture, one consisted of nameless carpenters, and the other consisted of illustrious inheritors of the traditions of such famous Buddhist sculptors as Unkei (d. 1223). From the modern viewpoint, the works of the experts seem lifeless when compared with the powerful, vital figures of phoenixes, dragons, and *baku* created by the carpenters. In comparison with the sculpture on the Kara-mon and the Main Hall, the Chinese lions on the Yomei-mon represent a different kind of workmanship. Though not superlative technically, the lions are quite alive with feeling. The crying lions, the happy ones, the ones about to sneeze, and so on remind us of the very human emotions of their makers.

In the *Tosho-gu Gozoei-cho*, the records of the shrine construction, we find that for the Main Hall and the Ishi-no-ma 168,991 ordinary workmen, 115,000 carpenter-sculptors, and 23,000 lumber haulers were employed; and that for the Worship Hall 140,404 ordinary workmen, 107,980 carpenter-sculptors, and 20,280 lumber haulers were employed. It is interesting that nearly forty percent of this vast working force was assigned to sculpture.

149. *Carved dragon underneath corner eaves, Yomei-mon gate. Nikko Tosho-gu.*

150. *Sculpture of the guardian of the night perched atop ridgecourse of Kara-mon gate. Bronze. Nikko Tosho-gu.*

Referring to other contemporary construction records, we see that the carpenters responsible for sculpture were skilled artisans just below the rank of master carpenter. Thus, being a skilled sculptor seems to have been a requirement in order to qualify as a master builder. From statements in the Kora family records we know that the master builder Kora Munehiro was a sculptor of great distinction.

It is probable that great sculptors from all over Japan gathered together and vied with each other in carving the sculptural ornamentation of the Tosho-gu. The famous Sleeping Cat carved into one of the frog-crotch struts of the corridor attached to the Yomei-mon is said to be the work of a master sculptor called Hidari Jingoro (Jingoro the Left-handed). There is little historical support for the existence of this man, but his name was known throughout the country. In records of the 1606

construction of the Katori Shrine in Sahara, Chiba Prefecture, mention is made of a "master sculptor from Sakai, a disciple of Kahei, the greatest practitioner of the fine-groove method."

FIGURES 39 AND 40. In the center of the Worship Hall there is a small hall; to its right is the Shogunal Chamber, used for the shogun's official visits, and to the left is the Cloistered Prince's Chamber, used by Gomizuno-o's son Morizumi, prince-abbot at the Rinno-ji. Four wall panels in the Shogunal Chamber are decorated with assembled sculptures of phoenixes among paulownia trees. The panels in the double-coved and coffered ceiling are also decorated with assembled wooden sculptures, including hollyhocks and phoenixes among other plants and animals. The Cloistered Prince's Chamber has hawks on the walls and celestial nymphs and chrysanthemums on the ceiling.

The carving in these rooms is probably the

151. Statue of Korean lion-dog guardian in front of Worship Hall, Oku-no-in precinct. Donated by Akimoto Yasutomo. Nikko Tosho-gu.

152. Worship Hall, Oku-no-in precinct. Nikko Tosho-gu.

most intricately wrought at the shrine. The materials used, according to the *Tosho-gu Gozoei-cho*, are eight types of wood: betel palm, Chinese quince, a variety of zelkova, rosewood, ironwood, sappanwood, black persimmon, and ebony. In ornamenting the walls of these rooms, the artists fully exploited the color and grain variations in the wood they used. Except for the zelkova, these woods were imported from tropical countries, and interestingly enough they are almost the same as the selection chosen for the Katsuradana.

Illustrated in Figure 40 is a detail of the third panel from the left in Figure 39. Since this particular panel was to provide the perfect background for the shogun's seat, the sculptor responsible for it was chosen from among the best artisans at the shrine. His exceptional skill is amply evident.

According to records of the Izumi family and

legends handed down at the Tosho-gu, a man named Izumi Chubei Yoshikazu, an artisan from Sakai, was mentioned as one of the creators of the assembled sculptures in the Worship Hall. The sculptor mentioned earlier in connection with the work at Katori Shrine was also from Sakai. During the Momoyama period, Sakai was a prosperous trading port noted for having nurtured such artists as the famous tea master Sen no Rikyu. It is indeed interesting that the same city produced excellent architectural sculptors, as well.

FIGURE 41. The Gokuro (Offering Corridor) is the hallway that begins in about the middle of the northern half of the east corridor and cuts through the Tamagaki wall to join the Ishi-no-ma. Called by a variety of names in old records, this is the passageway through which the daily offering to the enshrined deity is carried into the sanctuary. Offerings are also inspected here, and shelves were installed in the corridor's north wall for this purpose. Extending eastward from the southeast corner of the east corridor is another long hallway, which is also called Gokuro. Near this Gokuro is a storehouse for a variety of exquisite sacred implements and treasures offered to the spirit of Tokugawa Ieyasu. These two passageways, used only as accesses for offerings, were designed as branches of the main corridor.

The general architectural style of the Gokuro shown in Figure 41 is *wa-yo,* with the elegant air of shrine architecture apparent here and there. The beveled edges of the square pillars are also furrowed from top to bottom; the bracketing is in the simplified *wa-yo* style; and the rafters of the *karahafu-* gabled roof form the vaulted ceiling of the passageway. The color scheme is a tranquil combination of black, vermilion, and bluish green.

FIGURE 42. Unlike the Ishi-no-ma at the Tosho-gu, the Ai-no-ma at the Taiyu-in is not sunken: it has, instead, a narrow balcony on two sides. At left in Figure 42, where the narrow balcony along the Worship Hall joins the Ai-no-ma, is a door hinged in the Western manner. Above the door lintel is an excellent piece of openwork carving of the type usually called the "bamboo-joint transom." Near the ceiling, a boldly curved shrimp beam connects the pillars of the Worship Hall and the Ai-no-ma. The Ai-no-ma was designed so that walls, balconies, and beams contribute to a calm transition from the Main Hall to the Worship Hall.

As was previously noted, the design in this chamber exemplifies the architectural personality of the Taiyu-in. The technical proficiency and the sure sense of design shown in the reliefs of phoenixes and the elegant curvature of the shrimp beams represent the architectural taste of a time quite different from that which fostered the love of extravagance so evident at the Tosho-gu.

FIGURES 43–45. Before the 1616–17 construction of the Tosho-gu began, Todo Takatora (1556–1630), Titular Governor of Izumi (southern Osaka), and the priest Tenkai visited Nikko to survey the compound. Takatora, then a well-known castle planner, had previously built several castles for the

shogunate. Based on his original plans, during the 1634–36 reconstruction stone walls were built and other civil-engineering projects were carried out to bring the shrine to its present state. The arrangement of the stone walls as shown in the ground plan of the shrine opposite page 60 greatly resembles the wall plans favored for castles at that time and indicates the degree to which current castle design and construction techniques influenced the reconstruction.

The system of enclosing areas with stone walls at the Tosho-gu is suggestive of the concentric rings of walls so often seen in castles of that period. The boxlike stone wall around the former guardhouse and the jog in the stone wall in front of the Yomei-mon and its corridor are also strongly reminiscent of castle architecture.

The construction of stone walls and reservoirs for fire prevention is outstanding at the Tosho-gu. The previously mentioned Gokuro extended from the southeast corner of the Yomei-mon corridor is an excellent example of the quality of planning found here. At the juncture of this passageway and the corridor there is a thick stone wall with a heavy bronze door that seals off the passageway. Thanks to the protection afforded by this wall and door, when a fire broke out early in the nineteenth century, it destroyed only the Gokuro and a storehouse near it and did not spread to the adjoining corridor or the Yomei-mon. Another feature of the careful planning here is the plumbing and drainage system that services the whole compound. The water for the Washbasin Shed is supplied through a conduit fed by a siphon pump. Water pools, also part of the fire-prevention system, were built in the Oku-no-in and elsewhere during the 1634–36 reconstruction.

A tour of the Tosho-gu grounds reveals the impressive dexterity of designers and craftsmen in handling civil-engineering challenges in incorporating fire-prevention devices. Drainage spouts in the walls (Fig. 24), for example, are superbly designed. These are the work of silent contributors, so to speak, and are not immediately obvious but are nevertheless a delight to the observant eye.

In Figure 43 the Front Gate is seen from the

front approach, through the giant stone torii. This torii was built in 1618 and transported to Nikko by order of Kuroda Nagamasa (1568–1623), lord of the Fukuoka fief in Chikuzen Province in northern Kyushu. Roughly twenty-eight feet tall, it is made of granite in the Myojin style—that is to say, the ends of the upper beam rise gracefully, the lower beam passes through the mortised pillars, and a plaque is suspended between the two beams. This stoutly proportioned, stable torii is one of the finest torii constructed in its day.

Figure 44 shows the stone path and steps leading up to the Oku-no-in, where a treasury, a worship hall, and the Chinese-style gate called Inuki-mon are located. Tokugawa Ieyasu's remains are enshrined in the base of the bronze pagoda just beyond the Inuki-mon. Originally made of wood, this pagoda was rebuilt of stone during the 1634–36 construction. The stone pagoda collapsed during an earthquake in 1683 and, along with the Inuki-mon, was rebuilt in the bronze that visitors now see.

On either side of the stone stairway in front of the worship hall is a Korean lion-dog statue (Fig. 151). According to the inscriptions, the one on the left was donated by Akimoto Yasutomo; the one on the right, by Matsudaira Tadatsuna. In recognition of their meritorious service, these two supervising administrators for the 1634–36 construction were allowed to record their names on these statues so close to the sacred pagoda.

KATSURA: THE GARDEN AND TEAHOUSES

FIGURES 70–72. The focus of Katsura's garden, the pond, is said to be the remnant of one of the meanders of the Katsura River. The deep pond in the center of the villa is almost parallel to the river. In accordance with the overall plan of the villa, several other ponds were dug out around the original pond. The earth from the excavation was used to create the islets and hillocks of Katsura.

In Figure 70 the pond is seen across the bamboo moon-viewing platform in the Old Shoin. Visible in the center of this picture is the stone pagoda on the Shinsen islets in the middle of the pond. These

153. Plank bridge connecting residential quarters and Shinsen islets. Katsura Imperial Villa.

islets, with their grass and small pines, have a very soothing air about them. As if pictured in the mood of *yamato-e*, traditional Japanese-style painting, the islets embody the spirit of the sunny gardens of the Heian court.

The pathway of large steppingstones that leads from the Old Shoin veranda to the edge of the pond is crossed by a walkway made of smaller, carefully laid stones (Fig. 72). The huge steppingstones have a rough, natural beauty and perfectly complement the clean lines of the building.

This powerful impression disappears as one walks from the garden in front of the Old Shoin, past the Middle Shoin, and into the open area in front of the New Shoin. Figure 71 shows the part of this area just south of the Middle Shoin. In the upper right-hand part of this illustration, beyond the shoji, one can see on the ground a row of tiles that almost joins the steppingstones in the back-

154. Manji-tei pavilion. Katsura Imperial Villa.

planted on its front slope. The name Shoka-tei, or Flower Appreciation Pavilion, was probably prompted by the view of cherry blossoms on the slope below. The area around the Tatsuta River in Nara Prefecture is famous for its beautiful maples; and the other name of this teahouse, Tatsuta-ya, most likely indicates that it too was an excellent retreat for maple viewing in the fall.

This expanse of garden that unfolds before the *shoin* evokes a feeling quite different from that evoked by the Zen-inspired dry-landscape gardens of the middle ages. Here the small pine trees, cherry blossoms, and maples that are the beauty of Japanese nature are assembled in a grand setting. In Japan, creating a garden to encompass the distinct character of each of the four seasons was a technique used in Heian-period landscaping. While this tradition is observed at Katsura, the development of landscaping methods made it possible to continue the same tradition on a grander scale.

FIGURES 73 AND 74. The view from the Shokin-tei is one of a compact landscape with many vertical rocks concentrated within a small area. This is particularly true of the view to the north from the teahouse: the cobblestone-covered peninsula, the Ama no Hashidate miniature islands, the stone bridge, and the steppingstones in the water all embody the essence of gardening techniques of the past.

At left in the foreground of Figure 74, projecting into the pond, is the small peninsula covered with flat black cobblestones. At the tip of the peninsula is a small stone lantern. There are two opinions about the theme of this spit: one argument holds that the spit represents Takasago, a city in Hyogo Prefecture known for an excellent pine tree, and the other holds that it is Ya-u (night rain). Advocates of the Ya-u theory say that this spit represents a view of Karasaki, a promontory on the western shore of Lake Biwa, since the Night Rain of Karasaki has long been famous as one of the Eight Views of Omi (Shiga Prefecture). Supporters of the Takasago theory maintain that on or near this small spit there was once a large pine tree vying with that representing the Sumiyoshi Pine, which, it is said,

ground. These tiles separate the lawn on the outer side of the garden area from the moss on the inner side. The row of steppingstones in the center of the moss-covered area comes up under the eaves of the building. At left in this illustration, along the side of the building, is a graveled drain trench. The clear-cut, straight-line design of this section, along with the pleasing juxtaposition of the colors of grass, tile, moss, stone, and gravel, looks very modern and refined indeed.

In front of the *shoin* cluster there are several oddly shaped rock arrangements. But they are subordinate to the focal point of the view from the buildings: the expanse of the pond, the islets, and the hillocks beyond. At the highest point in the villa, atop the mound across the pond from the *shoin*, is the Shoka-tei teahouse; and at the foot of this mound is the Enrin-do. This man-made hillock, called "Flower Grove," has cherry trees

155. *Shinsen islets seen from Ichi-no-ma, Shokin-tei teahouse. Katsura Imperial Villa.*

156. *Nail cover in shape of daffodil used on* nageshi *beam, New Shoin. Katsura Imperial Villa.*

once stood on a site in the villa grounds, called Kame-no-o. Because the Takasago Pine and the Sumiyoshi Pine in Osaka have long been linked as an indivisible pair in Japanese literature, it is only a small step to associate the supposed Katsura pine with the Takasago Pine. The Takasago theorists also claim that "Ya-u" really referred to the bank just in front of the Shokin-tei. In any case, these are both latter-day speculations and cannot be verified.

The *suhama* (literally, "sandy beach" or "sands") illustrates one of the important techniques of the Heian landscape gardeners: spreading cobblestones on the bank of a pond to resemble a shoal. An early example of this technique has been discovered at the garden ruins of the Motsu-ji temple in Hiraizumi, Iwate Prefecture. Following this old tradition, the *suhama* at Katsura achieves fullness of expression in a much smaller area.

The islets off the tip of the peninsula, which are connected by stone bridges, are the Ama no Hashidate (Bridge of Heaven). The numerous rocks in the water around these little islands constitute the focus of expression. It is often pointed out that this scene is copied from an actual landscape—that is, it is in fact a representation of the Ama no Hashidate sandbar in northern Kyoto Prefecture. But the artist's intent in displaying the rock composition is more important than any relation this arrangement may have to a real site.

At extreme left in Figure 74, just in front of the teahouse, is a bridge made of a single slab of the famous Shirakawa granite from Kyoto. About nineteen feet long, with very little camber, the bridge has a very sharp, clean line. At one end of the bridge, steppingstones extend into the pond. Tradition has it that these stones were formerly used for the ritual hand washing before a tea ceremony, hence the name Nagare Chozu (literally, "washbasin with a stream"). Whether or not this tradition is true, the rocks are a pleasant sight even when seen simply as steppingstones in the pond.

As one can see in Figure 74, the thatched hipped-and-gabled roof of the Shokin-tei presents a very

157. *Interior of Ni-no-ma, Shokin-tei teahouse, showing* chigaidana *and* shitaji-mado. *Katsura Imperial Villa.*

pleasing and soothing appearance. To the left, in the gable facing the stone bridge, hangs a plaque that reads "Shokin." Going around to the south side (Fig. 73), one can clearly see the L shape of the building reflected in the roof. Cutting into the thatch roof is the tile roof of the adjoining lean-to, whose slightly orange wall contrasts beautifully with the brown thatch. We can well appreciate the artistry of a designer who created a roof that is so beautiful from every angle. The deep eaves over the earthen-floored area on two sides of the building also contribute to the composure of the overall appearance of this teahouse.

FIGURE 75. This is an interior view of the Ichi-no-ma in the Shokin-tei teahouse. Shown here is the blue-and-white Ichimatsu checkerboard pattern of the paper mounted on the *fusuma* at far left and on the tokonoma walls. The material is said to be fine crepe paper from Kaga, then a fief in what is now Ishikawa Prefecture. Prince Noritada's wife, Tomihime, was the daughter of the lord of Kaga, Maeda Toshitsune (d. 1658), which probably accounts for the paper. Among the superb design elements at Katsura, this vivid pattern is especially famous for its modern, cheerful feeling. The kind of sensitivity that produced this paper, along with the Old Kutani porcelain of Ishikawa Prefecture, must have had an important influence on the life of the times.

FIGURE 76. This interior view of the tearoom in the Shokin-tei shows the tea host's seat as seen from the tea guest's entrance. This tearoom is a *sanjo-daime*, that is, three tatami mats plus a *daime* (three-quarter mat for the host's seat). Although not shown in this illustration, to the left of the foreground there is also a three-quarter-mat tokonoma, which can be seen in Figure 88. In front of the host's seat is the *naka-bashira* (central post) made of unfinished wood, and the hearth is set into the floor beside the pillar. Beyond the partial wall joining the *naka-bashira* there is a window just above the floor, and there are shelves just above the window. The slanting ceiling above the host's seat is open timbered, and a skylight has been set into the roof. The combination of reeds and bamboo splits used in the horizontal ceiling near the tokonoma adds

the touch of a *wabi* (rustically simple) tearoom to this quiet interior.

The inclusion and placement of the *naka-bashira* and the *daime* mat indicate that this tearoom is faithful to the standards of its day, but in terms of design this is a superb example of how the skillful arrangement of doors and windows creates the atmosphere of a professional teahouse. Avoiding the austerity of the teahouses of Sen no Rikyu, this room is cheerful, subtle, and rich in variety. The sensitivity evident here is in perfect harmony with the lively, colorful tea gatherings popularized by Kobori Enshu.

FIGURE 77. In this view of the garden from the Ichi-no-ma in the Shokin-tei, the Ama no Hashidate islands are seen at right in the pond. To the left of these islands is a group of stones that look as if they are steps leading into the pond. These stones were once the foundation of a large vermilion-lacquered bridge; and according to old records, a branch path from the Miyuki-michi to the Shokin-tei led across this bridge. Imagining ourselves crossing this long-gone bridge on our way to the Shokin-tei, to our left we would command a view of the Ama no Hashidate stretching out parallel to the bridge—what a splendid sight that must have been. To the right we would contemplate the expanse of the pond and the view of the Shinsen islets—a sharp contrast to the rocky garden on the left. In effect, the bridge served as the boundary between these two very different types of scenery.

It is often stated that a vermilion-lacquered bridge would ill suit Katsura's spare design, but one cannot infer from this that the bridge was intended only as a temporary structure. As we have seen, from the very beginning it was planned as an integral part of the garden view from the Shokin-tei.

FIGURES 78 AND 79. Although the Ichi-no-ma of the Old Shoin is a formal sitting room, as Figure 79 shows, there are no shelves or decorative elements other than a tokonoma about two meters wide. Both beveled square pillars and those with bark left on the edges are used. The plain board ceiling is battened, and no decorative half beams are used to cover the simple beauty of the lintels.

The combination of two wooden doors and a single latticed shoji used in each bay of the outer wall is refreshing. Even when the doors are shut, their rough surfaces are still visible from the inside. The tokonoma walls are covered with paper decorated with paulownia flowers; however, the small wall between the lintels and the ceiling is only plastered. The *fusuma* that separate the Ichi-no-ma and the Ni-no-ma have black-lacquered frames; and above them is a particularly handsome mullioned transom.

Among *shoin*-style rooms of the period, this is one of the most modestly decorated. Had this room been built for official use, besides the tokonoma it would have had *chigaidana*, a *tsukeshoin*, and decorative beams above the lintels and near the ceiling; and the wooden doors outside would have had decorative rails added to them. The style of the Old Shoin, then, is not typical of the formal *shoin* style of Momoyama architecture but, rather, represents an adaptation for everyday living.

Elements of the teahouse have been incorporated into the design of the Ichi-no-ma. The use of pillars that still have bark on the edges, though inconspicuous, is one example. The omission of *chigaidana* next to the tokonoma is another. As one can see, an attempt was made to capture the simple, austere atmosphere of the teahouse. The construction methods are not particularly formal, either. The tenons of the tie beams protrude onto the veranda; no special effort has been made to cover or disguise them. Thus, in terms of design, carpentry, and finishing, this room is built in the very unassuming manner of an ordinary home.

FIGURES 80 AND 81. Behind the Ni-no-ma of the New Shoin is the oblong, six-mat room shown in Figure 81. Although it is called the Pantry, its function is not quite clear. The cabinets on the wall and its proximity to the kitchen suggest that it was a room for food or tea preparation. Seen at the far end of this corridorlike room is the imperial bedchamber, which has a strangely shaped cabinet called the Gyokendana, or Shelf for the Imperial Sword (Fig. 119), where the emperor's sword was stored at night. To the left of the Pantry in Figure 81 is the Ni-no-ma, whose *fusuma* have the famous door pulls shaped like the Chinese character for moon (Fig. 115). This motif derives from an ancient poem that described the natural setting of Katsura in the phrase "Katsura with its beautiful moon." The large elliptical window opening in the side wall of the tokonoma is said to be in the style of Kobori Enshu. Similar in shape to the "moon" door pulls, it was probably intended as a contrasting balance.

In the New Shoin, the design of the formal sitting rooms and the imperial bedchamber indicates carefully detailed planning and a rigid adherence to orthodox conventions. In and around the Pantry, however, the unpretentious merits of domestic architecture are well expressed.

FIGURES 82 AND 83. Over the bamboo fence just beyond the sitting rooms of the Shoi-ken, one can see fields. Looking through the sitting rooms of the Geppa-ro, across the pond one sees the Maple Hill in the distance. Just as the views from these teahouses are different, their interior designs are quite different.

The Shoi-ken gives one the impression of a rustic home. However, in the Naka-no-ma sitting room (Fig. 82), the velvet patches beneath the window display a vivid splash of colorful pattern. In the transom wall above the veranda, facing the pond, there are some round *shitaji-mado*, latticed windows. A calligraphic plaque here, bearing the word "Shoi" (the sensation of laughter), is said to have been inscribed by Toshihito's elder brother Ryojo, the cloistered prince at the Manju-in temple in Kyoto.

At the entrance to the earthen-floored area of the Geppa-ro (Fig. 83), one is first struck by the novelty of the ceiling. Under the open roof, the bark-covered logs used for the ridgepole and tie beams blend with bamboo, reeds, and the finished structural members. Similar combinations are seen at the teahouses Karakasa-tei (Umbrella Pavilion) and Shigure-tei (Autumn Rain Pavilion) at the Kodai-ji Zen temple in Kyoto. In the Geppa-ro the airiness of a pavilion has been skillfully harmonized with the design of the sitting rooms. Resting on the beam above the closed transom is a large plaque, dated 1605, depicting a foreign trading ship. Apparently this votive painting was originally offered at the Goryo Shrine in the village of Shimo Katsura, and no one knows when it was brought to the Geppa-ro. In any event, the fact that a painting of such an exotic and colorful sight as a foreign trading vessel should have been hung in a rustic teahouse reserved for simple tea ceremonies gives us an idea of the carefree atmosphere that must have prevailed at the time.

The wooden-floored area to the left of the earthen-floored area in Figure 83 is a kitchen, equipped with a hearth, an oven, shelves, and cupboards in the wall—fixtures that one would need for preparing tea or a meal. Kitchen equipment had never been considered as elements of architectural design. The fact that the kitchen fixtures are treated as integral parts of the architecture of the Geppa-ro indicates an attempt to incorporate into teahouse architecture the simple beauty of domestic architecture—an effort to pay due respect even to such functional components as kitchen fixtures.

FIGURE 84. To the left of the path branching off the Miyuki-michi (the path that once crossed the now lost vermilion-lacquered bridge) are some handsome steppingstones, which lead to a covered rest bench. In front of the bench there is a hillock called Cycas Hill, which is planted with cycas. A gift from the Shimazu family of Satsuma (in the western part of present-day Kagoshima Prefecture), these tropical plants represent a quest for novelty in the landscaping at Katsura.

The bench was used as the ceremonial waiting bench when tea ceremonies were performed in the Shokin-tei. About twelve feet long, the bench is protected by a thatch-roofed shelter and has a privy in back. In front of the bench is a stone walkway, at the end of which is a large stone step beside a square washbasin and a stone lantern (Fig. 84). The area was apparently used as a hand-washing site for tea ceremonies.

The washbasin is in the *tsukubai* (squatting) style—that is, it is so low that a person must crouch in order to use the water. The top of the stone is cut in the shape of two boxes, one nestled inside the other. The stone lantern has no pedestal; instead, its shaft is embedded directly in the ground. The

158 (above). Bamboo mullions at edge of veranda, Shoi-ken teahouse. Katsura Imperial Villa.

159 (left). Door pull in shape of oar used on wooden door, Shoi-ken teahouse. Katsura Imperial Villa.

160 (below). Door handle in shape of woman's hat used on wooden door, Gakki-no-ma. Katsura Imperial Villa.

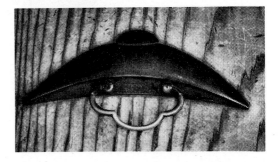

161. *Oribe-style stone lantern in front of Mikoshi-yose (Palanquin Approach). Katsura Imperial Villa.*

162. *Stone lantern with pyramidal roof in front of Shoi-ken teahouse. Katsura Imperial Villa.*

163. *"Snow-viewing lantern" in yard in front of New Shoin. Katsura Imperial Villa.*

roof and finial of the lantern are crumbling from exposure to the elements. In contrast to the stone lanterns at the Tosho-gu, many of which are large and formal, here at Katsura we find modest, informal lanterns that are suited to the natural style of the tea garden.

Informal washbasins and stone lanterns are scattered throughout the villa. Some of these basins and lanterns were actually intended to be used for washing and to provide illumination; but others were intended simply to be appreciated as one walked through the garden.

Among the famous washbasins at Katsura are the tall square one by the veranda on the right-hand side of the path leading to the Mikoshi-yose, the low, sickle-shaped one by the Geppa-ro, the large round one in front of the Shoka-tei (Fig. 164), and beneath the eaves of the Shoi-ken, one that has been hollowed out of living stone.

All along the paths in the garden one finds strangely sculpted old lanterns, all of them famous. Altogether there are seventeen lanterns, the most famous among them being the one by the Mikoshi-yose in Oribe's style, that is, with an embedded shaft (Fig. 161). The Keikyo (Bridge Illuminating) Lantern at the foot of the bridge crossing to the Shinsen islands and the "Christian" (Oribe-style) lantern at the tip of the cobblestone-covered peninsula (Fig. 87) have similar shapes. Simplified lanterns connected with the tea ceremony—that is, those from which the finial or shaft has been eliminated—include the Sanko Lantern (Fig. 127; composed of only the roof and the fire chamber) at the boat landing in front of the Shoi-ken and the Mizubotaru (Firefly) Lantern in front of the Shoka-tei.

Most of these lanterns have been placed with an eye to their proper function—to provide light for the boat landing, for a bridge, for paths on the hillocks, or for a washbasin. Not only can one clearly recall the Katsura of the daytime, but because of the lanterns one can also vividly imagine the Katsura of evening gatherings to enjoy the moon and fireflies.

164. *Washbasin in front of Shoka-tei teahouse. Katsura Imperial Villa.*

TITLES IN THE SERIES

Although the individual books in the series are designed as self-contained units, so that readers may choose subjects according to their personal interests, the series itself constitutes a full survey of Japanese art and will be of increasing reference value as it progresses. The following titles are listed in the same order, roughly chronological, as those of the original Japanese editions. Those marked with an asterisk (*) have already been published or will appear shortly. It is planned to publish the remaining titles at about the rate of eight a year, so that the English-language series will be complete in 1975.

The "weathermark" identifies this book as a production of John Weatherhill, Inc., publishers of fine books on Asia and the Pacific. Supervising editors: Rebecca Davis and Akito Miyamoto. Book design and typography: Meredith Weatherby. Layout of illustrations: Akito Miyamoto. Production supervision: Yutaka Shimoji. Composition: General Printing Co., Yokohama. Engraving and printing of color plates: Mitsumura Printing Co., Tokyo. Monochrome letterpress platemaking and printing and text printing: Toyo Printing Co., Tokyo. Binding: Makoto Binderies, Tokyo. The typeface used is Monotype Baskerville, with hand-set Optima for display.